PLANNED *Chaos*

PLANNED
Chaos

LUDWIG VON MISES

THE FOUNDATION FOR ECONOMIC EDUCATION, Inc.

IRVINGTON-ON-HUDSON, NEW YORK

The Author

Dr. Ludwig von Mises, now a member of the Staff of the Foundation for Economic Education, is the outstanding representative of the so-called "Austrian School" of economics. He is world-renowned for his research, writing, and teaching.

Publication of *The Theory of Money and Credit* in 1912 won him early recognition as one of Europe's foremost economists. Among his many other books and articles, one of his most important contributions is his *Socialism*, first published in 1922. However, he is best known in the United States for his works published in this country, notably *Omnipotent Government* (1944), *Bureaucracy* (1944), *Human Action* (1949), *Planning for Freedom* (1952), *The Anti-Capitalistic Mentality* (1956), *Theory and History* (1957), and *Epistemological Problems of Economics* (1960).

In 1926, Dr. Mises founded the Austrian Institute of Business Cycle Research. From then until the *Anschluss* of Austria by Germany in 1938, the Institute was one of the centers of economic and statistical research in Europe.

For more than twenty years, Dr. Mises taught economics at the University of Vienna. From 1934 to 1940, he occupied the chair of International Economic Relations at the Graduate Institute of International Studies at Geneva, Switzerland. He lectured as a guest at various universities and learned institutions of Great Britain, the United States, France, Italy, the Netherlands, and Mexico. At present he is a Visiting Professor of Economics at the Graduate School of Business Administration, New York University.

Foreword

A RECENT article by a well-known professor of economics, published in a leading economics journal, illustrates the chief threat to the economy of this and many other nations.

Most of the article was sound in conception and straightforward in statement. The author began by endorsing private property and capitalism. He pleaded for free markets for commodities and services, condemning monopoly by any group, whether "capital" or "labor." He demanded equality under the law, with protection for freedom of enterprise, production, and exchange. Only under such conditions, he said, could a people attain maximum prosperity and welfare.

So far, so good.

From that point, however, the author went on to advocate seizure (by government) of property and income from the most productive persons for the supposed benefit of the least productive. In other words, he advocated, not economic liberty, but a so-called "mixed system" for the professed purpose of "socializing" welfare. This system, he said, should be introduced slowly and quietly, by a variety of devices. He condemned the revolutionary socialists on the ground that bloodshed and violence were unnecessary. With patience and quiet perseverance, he contended, the change could be brought about peaceably.

On the surface, events appear to have borne out the contention that this expropriation or "socialization," of property might take place peaceably, that is, without armed revolution and civil war. But a closer view reveals that erosion of liberty throughout the world resulted in the two bloodiest wars of all history. And without violence at home? The destruction of liberty in America as elsewhere has been accomplished both by private violence and by the near irresistible force of the modern state.

9

This "easy, bloodless and non-violent" transition to socialism is the subject of *Planned Chaos*. Starting in Germany some 60 years or more ago, this "interventionism" has grown in popularity in one country after another throughout the world. As *Sozialpolitik*, the Welfare State, a New Deal, or Economic Planning, it is preached and promoted in churches, schools, farm organizations, and business associations as the "non-extremist, reasonable Middle Way." In *Planned Chaos* Professor Mises tells why the popularity of this policy is not a safe test of its soundness, why it fails in its avowed purposes, and what it does to the nations which pursue it.

Scientific study of interventionism has been the lifetime work of this eminent economist and scholar. It has also been a chief interest of the Austrian school of economics, of which Professor Mises is an outstanding representative. This school of economic thought had its origins about 90 years ago in the work of Carl Menger and Eugen Böhm-Bawerk. Among its present day leaders, in addition to Mises, are Friedrich von Hayek of the University of Chicago Committee on Social Thought, author of *The Road to Serfdom* and *The Constitution of Liberty*, and a growing number of younger economists in many countries.

This school of economic thought developed the "marginal utility" approach in the fields of value and distribution, a method of analysis which superseded the primitive and specious "labor cost," or "labor pain," theories. This development made the Austrian economists the leading critics of Marxian socialism and of the "socialists of the chair," who were mouthpieces in the German universities for Bismarck's welfare state and harbingers both of Social Democracy and Nazism.

In direct line and fruition of these years of scholarly effort was Professor Mises' treatise, *Socialism,* first published in 1922, and revised in 1932, both times in the German language. An English-language translation first appeared in 1936, a French translation in 1938, and a Spanish translation for which *Planned Chaos* was written as an epilogue in 1947. This epilogue also appears in the later edition of *Socialism,* published by Yale University Press in 1951.

Communist plotters, in the United States as elsewhere, are preparing for the conquest of political power. The discerning student, however, should consider how interventionism, under various enticing labels, is setting the stage for the final overthrow of the voluntary society, the market economy and constitutional government. *Planned Chaos,* by a world-famous expert, will prove a valuable aid to understanding in this field. It will help to explain the errors of those who, like the professor of economics referred to above, believe a system based on individual freedom can be "mixed" with socialism.

September 1961

LEONARD E. READ
of the Foundation Staff

Contents

Introductory Remarks

THE characteristic mark of this age of dictators, wars and revolutions is its anticapitalistic bias. Most governments and political parties are eager to restrict the sphere of private initiative and free enterprise. It is an almost unchallenged dogma that capitalism is done for and that the coming of all-round regimentation of economic activities is both inescapable and highly desirable.

Nonetheless capitalism is still very vigorous in the Western Hemisphere. Capitalist production has made very remarkable progress even in these last years. Methods of production were greatly improved. Consumers have been supplied with better and cheaper goods and with many new articles unheard of a short time ago. Many countries have expanded the size and improved the quality of their manufacturing. In spite of the anticapitalistic policies of all governments and of almost all political parties, the capitalist mode of production is still fulfilling its social function in supplying the consumers with more, better and cheaper goods.

It is certainly not a merit of governments, politicians and labor union officers that the standard of living is improving in the countries committed to the principle of private ownership of the means of production. Not offices and bureaucrats, but big business deserves credit for the fact that most of the families in the United States own a motorcar and a radio set. The increase in per capita consumption in America as compared with conditions a quarter of a century ago is not an achievement of laws and executive orders. It is an accomplishment of businessmen who enlarged the size of their factories or built new ones.

One must stress this point because our contemporaries are inclined to ignore it. Entangled in the superstitions of stateism and government omnipotence, they are exclusively preoccupied with governmental measures. They expect everything from authoritarian action and very little from the initiative of enterprising citizens. Yet, the only means to increase well-being is to increase the quantity of products. This is what business aims at.

It is grotesque that there is much more talk about the achievements of the Tennessee Valley Authority than about all the unprecedented and unparalleled achievements of American privately-operated processing industries. However, it was only the latter which enabled the United Nations to win the war.

The dogma that the State or the Government is the embodiment of all that is good and beneficial and that the individuals are wretched underlings, exclusively intent upon inflicting harm upon one another and badly in need of a guardian, is almost unchallenged. It is taboo to question it in the slightest way. He who proclaims the godliness of the State and the infallibility of its priests, the bureaucrats, is considered as an impartial student of the social sciences. All those raising objections are branded as biased and narrow-minded. The supporters of the new religion of statolatry are even more fanatical and intolerant than were the Mohammedan conquerors of Africa and Spain.

History will call our age the age of the dictators and tyrants. We have witnessed in the last years the fall of two of these inflated supermen. But the spirit which raised these knaves to autocratic power survives. It permeates textbooks and periodicals, it speaks through the mouths of teachers and politicians, it manifests itself in party programs and in plays and novels. As long as this spirit prevails there cannot be any hope of durable peace, of democracy,[1] the preservation of freedom or of a steady improvement in the nations' economic well-being.

---

[1] The term democracy, as I use it, means a system of government under which those ruled are in a position to determine, directly by plebiscite or indirectly by election, the mode in which the legislative and executive power is to be exercised and the selection of the supreme executives. Democracy is the very opposite of the Bolshevist, Fascist and Nazi principle according to which a group of self-appointed vanguardists has the right and the duty to seize the reins of government by violent action and to impose its own will upon the majority.

16

The Failure of Interventionism

NOTHING is more unpopular today than the free market economy, i.e., capitalism. Everything that is considered unsatisfactory in present-day conditions is charged to capitalism. The atheists make capitalism responsible for the survival of Christianity. But the papal encyclicals blame capitalism for the spread of irreligion and the sins of our contemporaries, and the Protestant churches and sects are no less vigorous in their indictment of capitalist greed. Friends of peace consider our wars as an offshoot of capitalist imperialism. But the adamant nationalist warmongers of Germany and Italy indicted capitalism for its "bourgeois" pacifism, contrary to human nature and to the inescapable laws of history. Sermonizers accuse capitalism of disrupting the family and fostering licentiousness. But the "progressives" blame capitalism for the preservation of allegedly outdated rules of sexual restraint. Almost all men agree that poverty is an outcome of capitalism. On the other hand many deplore the fact that capitalism, in catering lavishly to the wishes of people intent upon getting more amenities and a better living, promotes a crass materialism. These contradictory accusations of capitalism cancel one another. But the fact remains that there are few people left who would not condemn capitalism altogether.

Although capitalism is the economic system of modern Western civilization, the policies of all Western nations are guided by utterly anticapitalistic ideas. The aim of these interventionist policies is not to preserve capitalism, but to substitute a mixed economy for it. It is assumed that this mixed economy is neither capitalism nor socialism. It is described as a third system, as far from capitalism as it is from socialism. It is alleged that it stands midway be-

17

tween socialism and capitalism, retaining the advantages of both and avoiding the disadvantages inherent in each.

More than half a century ago the outstanding man in the British socialist movement, Sidney Webb, declared that the socialist philosophy is "but the conscious and explicit assertion of principles of social organization which have been already in great part unconsciously adopted." And he added that the economic history of the nineteenth century was "an almost continuous record of the progress of socialism."[1] A few years later an eminent British statesman, Sir William Harcourt, stated: "We are all socialists now."[2] When in 1913 an American, Elmer Roberts, published a book on the economic policies of the Imperial Government of Germany as conducted since the end of the seventies, he called them "monarchical socialism."[3]

However, it was not correct simply to identify interventionism and socialism. There are many supporters of interventionism who consider it as the most appropriate method to realize — step by step — full socialism. But there are also many interventionists who are not outright socialists; they aim at the establishment of the mixed economy as a permanent system of economic management. They endeavor to restrain, to regulate and to "improve" capitalism by government interference with business and by labor unionism.

In order to comprehend the working of interventionism and of the mixed economy it is necessary to clarify two points:

First: If within a society based on private ownership of the means of production some of these means are owned and operated by the government or by municipalities, this still does not make for a mixed system which would combine socialism and private ownership. As long as only certain individual enterprises are publicly controlled, the characteristics of the market economy determining economic activity remain essentially unimpaired. The publicly owned enterprises, too, as buyers of raw materials, semifinished goods, and labor and as sellers of goods and services, must

---

[1] Sidney Webb in *Fabian Essays in Socialism,* first published in 1889 (American edition, New York 1891, p. 4).
[2] Cf. G. M. Trevelyan, *A Shortened History of England* (London 1942), p. 510.
[3] Elmer Roberts, *Monarchical Socialism in Germany,* (New York 1913).

fit into the mechanism of the market economy. They are subject to the law of the market; they have to strive after profits or, at least, to avoid losses. When it is attempted to mitigate or to eliminate this dependence by covering the losses of such enterprises with subsidies out of public funds, the only result is a shifting of this dependence somewhere else. This is because the means for the subsidies have to be raised somewhere. They may be raised by collecting taxes. But the burden of such taxes has its effects on the public, not on the government collecting the tax. It is the market, and not the revenue department, which decides upon whom the burden of the tax falls and how it affects production and consumption. The market and its inescapable law are supreme.

Second: There are two different patterns for the realization of socialism. The one pattern — we may call it the Marxian or Russian pattern — is purely bureaucratic. All economic enterprises are departments of the government just as the administration of the army and the navy or the postal system. Every single plant, shop, or farm, stands in the same relation to the superior central organization as does a post office to the office of the Postmaster General. The whole nation forms one single labor army with compulsory service; the commander of this army is the chief of state.

The second pattern — we may call it the German or *Zwangswirtschaft* system[1] — differs from the first one in that it, seemingly and nominally, maintains private ownership of the 'means of production, entrepreneurship, and market exchange. So-called entrepreneurs do the buying and selling, pay the workers, contract debts and pay interest and amortization. But they are no longer entrepreneurs. In Nazi Germany they were called shop managers or *Betriebsführer*. The government tells these seeming entrepreneurs what and how to produce, at what prices and from whom to buy, at what prices and to whom to sell. The government decrees at what wages laborers should work and to whom and under what terms the capitalists should entrust their funds. Market exchange is but a sham. As all prices, wages, and interest rates are fixed by the authority, they are prices, wages, and interest rates in

---

[1] *Zwang* means compulsion, *Wirtschaft* means economy. The English-language equivalent for *Zwangswirtschaft* is something like compulsory economy.

appearance only; in fact they are merely quantitative terms in the authoritarian orders determining each citizen's income, consumption, and standard of living. The authority, not the consumers, directs production. The central board of production management is supreme; all citizens are nothing else but civil servants. This is socialism, with the outward appearance of capitalism. Some labels of the capitalistic market economy are retained, but they signify here something entirely different from what they mean in the market economy.

It is necessary to point out this fact to prevent a confusion of socialism and interventionism. The system of the hampered market economy, or interventionism, differs from socialism by the very fact that it is still market economy. The authority seeks to influence the market by the intervention of its coercive power, but it does not want to eliminate the market altogether. It desires that production and consumption should develop along lines different from those prescribed by the unhindered market, and it wants to achieve its aim by injecting into the working of the market orders, commands, and prohibitions for whose enforcement the police power and its apparatus of coercion and compulsion stand ready. But these are isolated interventions; their authors assert that they do not plan to combine these measures into a completely integrated system which regulates all prices, wages, and interest rates, and which thus places full control of production and consumption in the hands of the authorities.

However, all the methods of interventionism are doomed to failure. This means: the interventionist measures must needs result in conditions which *from the point of view of their own advocates* are more unsatisfactory than the previous state of affairs they were designed to alter. These policies are therefore contrary to purpose.

Minimum wage rates, whether enforced by government decree or by labor union pressure and compulsion, are useless if they fix wage rates at the market level. But if they try to raise wage rates above the level which the unhampered labor market would have determined, they result in permanent unemployment of a great part of the potential labor force.

Government spending cannot create additional jobs. If the gov-

20

ernment provides the funds required by taxing the citizens or by borrowing from the public, it abolishes on the one hand as many jobs as it creates on the other. If government spending is financed by borrowing from the commercial banks, it means credit expansion and inflation. If in the course of such an inflation the rise in commodity prices exceeds the rise in nominal wage rates, unemployment will drop. But what makes unemployment shrink, is precisely the fact that real wage rates are falling.

The inherent tendency of capitalist evolution is to raise real wage rates steadily. This is the effect of the progressive accumulation of capital by means of which technological methods of production are improved. There is no means by which the height of wage rates can be raised for all those eager to earn wages other than through the increase of the per capita quota of capital invested. Whenever the accumulation of additional capital stops, the tendency toward a further increase in real wage rates comes to a standstill. If capital consumption is substituted for an increase in capital available, real wage rates must drop temporarily until the checks on a further increase in capital are removed. Government measures which retard capital accumulation or lead to capital consumption — such as confiscatory taxation — are therefore detrimental to the vital interests of the workers.

Credit expansion can bring about a temporary boom. But such a fictitious prosperity must end in a general depression of trade, a slump.

It can hardly be asserted that the economic history of the last decades has run counter to the pessimistic predictions of the economists. Our age has to face great economic troubles. But this is not a crisis of capitalism. It is the crisis of interventionism, of policies designed to improve capitalism and to substitute a better system for it.

No economist ever dared to assert that interventionism could result in anything else than in disaster and chaos. The advocates of interventionism — foremost among them the Prussian Historical School and the American Institutionalists — were not economists. On the contrary. In order to promote their plans they flatly denied that there is any such thing as economic law. In their opinion governments are free to achieve all they aim at without being re-

21

strained by an inexorable regularity in the sequence of economic phenomena. Like the German socialist Ferdinand Lassalle, they maintain that the State is God.

The interventionists do not approach the study of economic matters with scientific disinterestedness. Most of them are driven by an envious resentment against those whose incomes are larger than their own. This bias makes it impossible for them to see things as they really are. For them the main thing is not to improve the conditions of the masses, but to harm the entrepreneurs and capitalists even if this policy victimizes the immense majority of the people.

In the eyes of the interventionists the mere existence of profits is objectionable. They speak of profit without dealing with its corollary, loss. They do not comprehend that profit and loss are the instruments by means of which the consumers keep a tight rein on all entrepreneurial activities. It is profit and loss that make the consumers supreme in the direction of business. It is absurd to contrast production for profit and production for use. On the unhampered market a man can earn profits only by supplying the consumers in the best and cheapest way with the goods they want to use. Profit and loss withdraw the material factors of production from the hands of the inefficient and place them in the hands of the more efficient. It is their social function to make a man the more influential in the conduct of business the better he succeeds in producing commodities for which people scramble. The consumers suffer, when the laws of the country prevent the most efficient entrepreneurs from expanding the sphere of their activities. What made some enterprises develop into "big business" was precisely their success in filling best the demand of the masses.

Anticapitalistic policies sabotage the operation of the capitalist system of the market economy. The failure of interventionism does not demonstrate the necessity of adopting socialism. It merely exposes the futility of interventionism. All those evils which the self-styled "progressives" interpret as evidence of the failure of capitalism are the outcome of their allegedly beneficial interference with the market. Only the ignorant, wrongly identifying interventionism and capitalism, believe that the remedy for these evils is socialism.

2

The Dictatorial, Anti-democratic and
Socialist Character of Interventionism

MANY advocates of interventionism are bewildered when one tells them that in recommending interventionism they themselves are fostering antidemocratic and dictatorial tendencies and the establishment of totalitarian socialism. They protest that they are sincere believers in democracy and opposed to tyranny and socialism. What they aim at is only the improvement of the conditions of the poor. They say that they are driven by considerations of social justice and favor a fairer distribution of income precisely because they are intent upon preserving capitalism and its political corollary or superstructure, viz., democratic government.

What these people fail to realize is that the various measures they suggest are not capable of bringing about the beneficial results aimed at. On the contrary they produce a state of affairs which from the point of view of their advocates is worse than the previous state which they were designed to alter. If the government, faced with this failure of its first intervention, is not prepared to undo its interference with the market and to return to a free economy, it must add to its first measure more and more regulations and restrictions. Proceeding step by step on this way it finally reaches a point in which all economic freedom of individuals has disappeared. Then socialism of the German pattern, the *Zwangswirtschaft* of the Nazis, emerges.

We have already mentioned the case of minimum wage rates. Let us illustrate the matter further by an analysis of a typical case of price control.

If the government wants to make it possible for poor parents to give more milk to their children, it must buy the milk at the market price and sell it to those poor people with a loss at a cheaper rate; the loss may be covered from the means collected by taxation. But if the government simply fixes the price of milk at a lower rate than the market, the results obtained will be contrary to the aims of the government. The marginal producers will, in order to avoid losses, go out of the business of producing and selling milk. There will be less milk available for the consumers, not more. This outcome is contrary to the government's intentions. The government interfered because it considered milk as a vital necessity. It did not want to restrict its supply.

Now the government has to face the alternative: either to refrain from any endeavors to control prices or to add to its first measure a second one, i.e., to fix the prices of the factors of production necessary for the production of milk. Then the same story repeats itself on a remoter plane; the government has again to fix the prices of the factors of production necessary for the production of those factors of production which are needed for the production of milk. Thus the government has to go further and further, fixing the prices of all the factors of production — both human (labor) and material — and forcing every entrepreneur and every worker to continue work at these prices and wages. No branch of production can be omitted from this all-round fixing of prices and wages and this general order to continue production. If some branches of production were left free, the result would be a shifting of capital and labor to them and a corresponding fall of the supply of the goods whose prices the government had fixed. However, it is precisely these goods which the government considers as especially important for the satisfaction of the needs of the masses.

But when this state of all-round control of business is achieved, the market economy has been replaced by a system of planned economy, by socialism. Of course, this is not the socialism of immediate state management of every plant by the government as in Russia, but the socialism of the German or Nazi pattern.

Many people were fascinated by the alleged success of German price control. They said: You have only to be as brutal and ruthless as the Nazis and you will succeed in controlling prices. What these people, eager to fight Nazism by adopting its methods, did not see was that the Nazis did not enforce price control within a market society, but that they established a full socialist system, a totalitarian commonwealth.

Price control is contrary to purpose if it is limited to some commodities only. It cannot work satisfactorily within a market economy. If the government does not draw from this failure the conclusion that it must abandon all attempts to control prices, it must go further and further until it substitutes socialist all-round planning for the market economy.

Production can either be directed by the prices fixed on the market by the buying and by the abstention from buying on the part of the public. Or it can be directed by the government's central board of production management. There is no third solution available. There is no third social system feasible which would be neither market economy nor socialism. Government control of only a part of prices must result in a state of affairs which — without any exception — everybody considers as absurd and contrary to purpose. Its inevitable result is chaos and social unrest.

It is this that the economists have in mind in referring to economic law and asserting that interventionism is contrary to economic law.

In the market economy the consumers are supreme. Their buying and their abstention from buying ultimately determines what the entrepreneurs produce and in what quantity and quality. It determines directly the prices of the consumers' goods and indirectly the prices of all producers' goods, viz., labor and material factors of production. It determines the emergence of profits and losses and the formation of the rate of interest. It determines every individual's income. The focal point of the market economy is the market, i.e., the process of the formation of commodity prices, wage rates and interest rates and their derivatives, profits and losses. It makes all men in their capacity as producers responsible to the consumers. This dependence is direct with entrepreneurs, capitalists, farmers and professional men, and indirect with people working for salaries and wages. The market adjusts the efforts of all those engaged in supplying the needs of the consumers to the wishes of those for whom they produce, the consumers. It subjects production to consumption.

The market is a democracy in which every penny gives a right to vote. It is true that the various individuals have not the same power to vote. The richer man casts more ballots than the poorer fellow. But to be rich and to earn a higher income is, in the market economy, already the outcome of a previous election. The only means to acquire wealth and to preserve it, in a market economy not adulterated by government-made privileges and restrictions, is to serve the consumers in the best and cheapest way. Capitalists and landowners who fail in this regard suffer losses. If they do not change their procedure, they lose their wealth and become poor. It is the consumers who make poor people rich and rich people poor. It is the consumers who fix the wages of a movie star and an opera singer at a higher level than those of a welder or an accountant.

Every individual is free to disagree with the outcome of an election campaign or of the market process. But in a democracy he has no other means to alter things than persuasion. If a man were to say: "I do not like the mayor elected by majority vote; therefore I ask the government to replace him by the man I prefer," one would hardly call him a democrat. But if the same claims are raised with regard to the market, most people are too dull to discover the dictatorial aspirations involved.

The consumers have made their choices and determined the income of the shoe manufacturer, the movie star and the welder. Who is Professor X to arrogate to himself the privilege of overthrowing their decision? If he were not a potential dictator, he would not ask the government to interfere. He would try to persuade his fellow-citizens to increase their demand for the products of the welders and to reduce their demand for shoes and pictures.

The consumers are not prepared to pay for cotton prices which would render the marginal farms, i.e., those producing under the least favorable conditions, profitable. This is very unfortunate indeed for the farmers concerned; they must discontinue growing cotton and try to integrate themselves in another way into the whole of production.

But what shall we think of the statesman who interferes by compulsion in order to raise the price of cotton above the level it would reach on the free market? What the interventionist aims at is the substitution of police pressure for the choice of the con-

26

sumers. All this talk: the state should do this or that, ultimately means: the police should force consumers to behave otherwise than they would behave spontaneously. In such proposals as: let *us* raise farm prices, let *us* raise wage rates, let *us* lower profits, let *us* curtail the salaries of executives, the *us* ultimately refers to the police. Yet, the authors of these projects protest that they are planning for freedom and industrial democracy.

In most non-socialist countries the labor unions are granted special rights. They are permitted to prevent non-members from working. They are allowed to call a strike and, when on strike, are virtually free to employ violence against all those who are prepared to continue working, viz., the strikebreakers. This system assigns an unlimited privilege to those engaged in vital branches of industry. Those workers whose strike cuts off the supply of water, light, food and other necessities are in a position to obtain all they want at the expense of the rest of the population. It is true that in the United States their unions have up to now exercised some moderation in taking advantage of this opportunity. Other American unions and the European unions have been less cautious. They are intent upon enforcing wage increases without bothering about the disaster inevitably resulting.

The interventionists are not shrewd enough to realize that labor union pressure and compulsion are absolutely incompatible with any system of social organization. The union problem has no reference whatsoever to the right of citizens to associate with one another in assemblies and associations; no democratic country denies its citizens this right. Neither does anybody dispute a man's right to stop work and to go on strike. The only question is whether or not the unions should be granted the privilege of resorting with impunity to violence. This privilege is no less incompatible with socialism than with capitalism. No social cooperation under the division of labor is possible when some people or unions of people are granted the right to prevent by violence and the threat of violence other people from working. When enforced by violence, a strike in vital branches of production or a general strike are tantamount to a revolutionary destruction of society.

A government abdicates if it tolerates any non-governmental agency's use of violence. If the government forsakes its monopoly

27

of coercion and compulsion, anarchic conditions result. If it were true that a democratic system of government is unfit to protect unconditionally every individual's right to work in defiance of the orders of a union, democracy would be doomed. Then dictatorship would be the only means to preserve the division of labor and to avoid anarchy. What generated dictatorship in Russia and Germany was precisely the fact that the mentality of these nations made suppression of union violence unfeasible under democratic conditions. The dictators abolished strikes and thus broke the spine of labor unionism. There is no question of strikes in the Soviet empire.

It is illusory to believe that arbitration of labor disputes could bring the unions into the framework of the market economy and make their functioning compatible with the preservation of domestic peace. Judicial settlement of controversies is feasible if there is a set of rules available, according to which individual cases can be judged. But if such a code is valid and its provisions are applied to the determination of the height of wage rates, it is no longer the market which fixes them, but the code and those who legislate with regard to it. Then the government is supreme and no longer the consumers buying and selling on the market. If no such code exists, a standard according to which a controversy between employers and employees could be decided is lacking. It is vain to speak of "fair" wages in the absence of such a code. The notion of fairness is nonsensical if not related to an established standard. In practice, if the employers do not yield to the threats of the unions, arbitration is tantamount to the determination of wage rates by the government-appointed arbitrator. Peremptory authoritarian decision is substituted for the market price. The issue is always the same: the government *or* the market. There is no third solution.

Metaphors are often very useful in elucidating complicated problems and in making them comprehensible to less intelligent minds. But they become misleading and result in nonsense if people forget that every comparison is imperfect. It is silly to take metaphorical idioms literally and to deduce from their interpretation features of the object one wished to make more easily understandable by their use. There was no harm in the economists' description of the operation of the market as *automatic* and in their custom of speaking of the *anonymous* forces operating on the market. They could not anticipate that anybody would be so stupid as to take these metaphors literally.

No "automatic" and "anonymous" forces actuate the "mechanism" of the market. The only factors directing the market and determining prices are purposive acts of men. There is no automatism; there are men consciously aiming at ends chosen and deliberately resorting to definite means for the attainment of these ends. There are no mysterious mechanical forces; there is only the will of every individual to satisfy his demand for various goods. There is no anonymity; there are you and I and Bill and Joe and all the rest. And each of us is engaged both in production and consumption. Each contributes his share to the determination of prices.

The dilemma is not between automatic forces and planned action. It is between the democratic process of the market in which every individual has his share and the exclusive rule of a dictatorial body. Whatever people do in the market economy, is the execution of their own plans. In this sense every human action means planning. What those calling themselves planners advocate is not the substitution of planned action for letting things go. It is the substitution of the planner's own plan for the plans of his fellowmen. The planner is a potential dictator who wants to deprive all other people of the power to plan and act according to their own plans. He aims at one thing only: the exclusive absolute preeminence of his own plan.

It is no less erroneous to declare that a government that is not socialistic has no plan. Whatever a government does is the execution of a plan, i.e., of a design. One may disagree with such a plan. But one must not say that it is not a plan at all. Professor Wesley C. Mitchell maintained that the British liberal government "planned to have no plan."[1] However, the British government in the liberal age certainly had a definite plan. Its plan was private ownership of the means of production, free initiative and market economy. Great Britain was very prosperous indeed under this plan which according to Professor Mitchell is "no plan."

The planners pretend that their plans are scientific and that

---

[1] Cf. Wesley C. Mitchell, *The Social Sciences and National Planning* (in: *Planned Society*, ed. by Findlay Mackenzie, New York 1937), p. 112.

there cannot be disagreement with regard to them among well-intentioned and decent people. However, there is no such thing as a scientific *ought*. Science is competent to establish what *is*. It can never dictate what ought to be and what ends people should aim at. It is a fact that men disagree in their value judgments. It is insolent to arrogate to oneself the right to overrule the plans of other people and to force them to submit to the plan of the planner. Whose plan should be executed? The plan of the CIO or those of any other group? The plan of Trotsky or that of Stalin? The plan of Hitler or that of Strasser?

When people were committed to the idea that in the field of religion only one plan must be adopted, bloody wars resulted. With the acknowledgment of the principle of religious freedom these wars ceased. The market economy safeguards peaceful economic cooperation because it does not use force upon the economic plans of the citizens. If one masterplan is to be substituted for the plans of each citizen, endless fighting must emerge. Those who disagree with the dictator's plan have no other means to carry on than to defeat the despot by force of arms.

It is an illusion to believe that a system of planned socialism could be operated according to democratic methods of government. Democracy is inextricably linked with capitalism. It cannot exist where there is planning. Let us refer to the words of the most eminent of the contemporary advocates of socialism. Professor Harold Laski declared that the attainment of power by the British Labor Party in the normal parliamentary fashion must result in a radical transformation of parliamentary government. A socialist administration needs "guarantees" that its work of transformation would not be "disrupted" by repeal in event of its defeat at the polls. Therefore the suspension of the Constitution is "inevitable."[1] How pleased would Charles I and George III have been if they had known the books of Professor Laski!

Sidney and Beatrice Webb (Lord and Lady Passfield) tell us that "in any corporate action a loyal unity of thought is so important that, if anything is to be achieved, public discussion must be suspended between the promulgation of the decision and the ac-

---

[1] Cf. Laski, *Democracy in Crisis*, (Chapel Hill 1933), pp. 87-88.

complishment of the task." Whilst "the work is in progress" any expression of doubt, or even of fear that the plan will not be successful, is "an act of disloyalty, or even of treachery."[1] Now as the process of production never ceases and some work is always in progress and there is always something to be achieved, it follows that a socialist government must never concede any freedom of speech and the press. "A loyal unity of thought," what a high-sounding circumlocution for the ideals of Philip II and the inquisition! In this regard another eminent admirer of the Soviets, Mr. T. G. Crowther, speaks without any reserve. He plainly declares that inquisition is "beneficial to science when it protects a rising class,"[2] i.e., when Mr. Crowther's friends resort to it. Hundreds of similar dicta could be quoted.

In the Victorian age, when John Stuart Mill wrote his essay *On Liberty,* such views as those held by Professor Laski, Mr. and Mrs. Webb and Mr. Crowther were called reactionary. Today they are called "progressive" and "liberal." On the other hand people who oppose the suspension of parliamentary government and of the freedom of speech and the press and the establishment of inquisition are scorned as "reactionaries," as "economic royalists" and as "Fascists."

Those interventionists who consider interventionism as a method of bringing about full socialism step by step are at least consistent. If the measures adopted fail to achieve the beneficial results expected and end in disaster, they ask for more and more government interference until the government has taken over the direction of all economic activities. But those interventionists who look at interventionism as a means of improving capitalism and thereby preserving it are utterly confused.

In the eyes of these people all the undesired and undesirable effects of government interference with business are caused by capitalism. The very fact that a governmental measure has brought about a state of affairs which they dislike is for them a justification of further measures. They fail, for instance, to realize that the role monopolistic schemes play in our time is the effect of government

[1] Cf. Sidney and Beatrice Webb, *Soviet Communism: A New Civilization?* (New York 1936), Vol. II, pp. 1038-1039.
[2] Cf. T. G. Crowther, *Social Relations of Science* (London 1941), p. 333.

interference such as tariffs and patents. They advocate government action for the prevention of monopoly. One could hardly imagine a more unrealistic idea. For the governments whom they ask to fight monopoly are the same governments who are devoted to the principle of monopoly. Thus, the American New Deal Government embarked upon a thorough-going monopolistic organization of every branch of American business, by the NRA, and aimed at organizing American farming as a vast monopolistic scheme, restricting farm output for the sake of substituting monopoly prices for the lower market prices. It was a party to various international commodity control agreements the undisguised aim of which was to establish international monopolies of various commodities. The same is true of all other governments. The Union of Soviet Socialist Republics was also a party to some of these intergovernmental monopolistic conventions.[1] Its repugnance for collaboration with the capitalistic countries was not so great as to cause it to miss any opportunity for fostering monopoly.

The program of this self-contradictory interventionism is dictatorship, supposedly to make people free. But the liberty its supporters advocate is liberty to do the "right" things, i.e., the things they themselves want to be done. They are not only ignorant of the economic problems involved. They lack the faculty of logical thinking.

The most absurd justification of interventionism is provided by those who look upon the conflict between capitalism and socialism as if it were a contest over the distribution of income. Why should not the propertied classes be more compliant? Why should they not accord to the poor workers a part of their ample revenues? Why should they oppose the government's design to raise the share of the underprivileged by decreeing minimum wage rates and maximum prices and by cutting profits and interest rates down to a "fairer" level? Pliability in such matters, they say, would take the wind from the sails of the radical revolutionaries and preserve capitalism. The worst enemies of capitalism, they say, are those intransigent doctrinaires whose excessive advocacy of economic

---

[1] Cf. the collection of these conventions, published by The International Labor Office under the title *Intergovernmental Commodity Control Agreements.* (Montreal, 1943).

freedom, of laissez-faire and Manchesterism renders vain all attempts to come to a compromise with the claims of labor. These adamant reactionaries are alone responsible for the bitterness of contemporary party strife and the implacable hatred it generates. What is needed is the substitution of a constructive program for the purely negative attitude of the economic royalists. And, of course, "constructive" is in the eyes of these people only interventionism.

However, this mode of reasoning is entirely vicious. It takes for granted that the various measures of government interference with business will attain those beneficial results which their advocates expect from them. It blithely disregards all that economics says about their futility in attaining the ends sought and their unavoidable and undesirable consequences. The question is not whether minimum wage rates are fair or unfair, but whether or not they bring about unemployment of a part of those eager to work. By calling these measures just, the interventionist does not refute the objections raised against their expediency by the economists. He merely displays ignorance of the question at issue.

The conflict between capitalism and socialism is not a contest between two groups of claimants concerning the size of the portions to be allotted to each of them out of a definite supply of goods. It is a dispute concerning what system of social organization best serves human welfare. Those fighting socialism do not reject socialism because they envy the workers' benefits they could allegedly derive from the socialist mode of production. They fight socialism precisely because they are convinced that it would harm the masses in reducing them to the status of poor serfs entirely at the mercy of irresponsible dictators.

In this conflict of opinions everybody must make up his mind and take a definite stand. Everybody must side either with the advocates of economic freedom or with those of totalitarian socialism. One cannot evade this dilemma by adopting an allegedly middle-of-the-road position, namely interventionism. For interventionism is neither a middle way nor a compromise between capitalism and socialism. It is a third system. It is a system the absurdity and futility of which is agreed upon not only by all economists but even by the Marxians.

There is no such thing as an "excessive" advocacy of economic freedom. On the one hand, production can be directed by the efforts of each individual to adjust his conduct so as to fill the most urgent wants of the consumers in the most appropriate way. This is the market economy. On the other hand, production can be directed by authoritarian decree. If these decrees concern only some isolated items of the economic structure, they fail to attain the ends sought and their own advocates do not like their outcome. If they come up to all-round regimentation, they mean totalitarian socialism.

Men must choose between the market economy and socialism. The state can preserve the market economy in protecting life, health and private property against violent or fraudulent aggression; or it can itself control the conduct of all production activities. Some agency must determine what should be produced. If it is not the consumers by means of demand and supply on the market, it must be the government by compulsion.

3

Socialism and Communism

IN the terminology of Marx and Engels the words communism and socialism are synonymous. They are alternately applied without any distinction between them. The same was true for the practice of all Marxian groups and sects until 1917. The political parties of Marxism which considered the *Communist Manifesto* as the unalterable gospel of their doctrine called themselves *socialist* parties. The most influential and most numerous of these parties, the German party, adopted the name Social Democratic Party. In Italy, in France and in all other countries in which Marxian parties already played a role in political life before 1917, the term *socialist* likewise superseded the term *communist*. No Marxian ever ventured, before 1917, to distinguish between communism and socialism.

In 1875, in his Criticism of the Gotha Program of the German Social Democratic Party, Marx distinguished between a lower (earlier) and a higher (later) phase of the future communist society. But he did not reserve the name of communism to the higher phase and did not call the lower phase socialism as differentiated from communism.

One of the fundamental dogmas of Marx is that socialism is bound to come "with the inexorability of a law of nature." Capitalist production begets its own negation and establishes the socialist system of public ownership of the means of production. This process "executes itself through the operation of the inherent laws of capitalist production."[1] It is independent of the wills of people.[2] It is impossible for men to accelerate it, to delay it or to hinder it.

---

[1] Marx, *Das Kapital* (7th edition, Hamburg 1914), Vol. I., p. 728.
[2] Marx, *Zur Kritik der politischen Oekonomie*, ed. by Kautsky (Stuttgart 1897), p. XI.

For "no social system ever disappears before all the productive forces are developed for the development of which it is broad enough, and new higher methods of production never appear before the material conditions of their existence have been hatched out in the womb of previous society."[1]

This doctrine is, of course, irreconcilable with Marx's own political activities and with the teachings he advanced for the justification of these activities. Marx tried to organize a political party which by means of revolution and civil war should accomplish the transition from capitalism to socialism. The characteristic feature of their parties was, in the eyes of Marx and all Marxian doctrinaires, that they were revolutionary parties invariably committed to the idea of violent action. Their aim was to rise in rebellion, to establish the dictatorship of the proletarians and to exterminate mercilessly all bourgeois. The deeds of the Paris Communards in 1871 were considered as the perfect model of such a civil war. The Paris revolt, of course, had lamentably failed. But later uprisings were expected to succeed.[2]

However, the tactics applied by the Marxian parties in various European countries were irreconcilably opposed to each of these two contradictory varieties of the teachings of Karl Marx. They did not place confidence in the inevitability of the coming of socialism. Neither did they trust in the success of a revolutionary upheaval. They adopted the method of parliamentary action. They solicited votes in election campaigns and sent their delegates into the parliaments. They "degenerated" into democratic parties. In the parliaments they behaved like other parties of the opposition. In some countries they entered into temporary alliances with other parties, and occasionally socialist members sat in the cabinets. Later, after the end of the first World War, the socialist parties became paramount in many parliaments. In some countries they ruled exclusively, in others in close cooperation with "bourgeois" parties.

It is true, that these domesticated socialists before 1917 never abandoned lip service to the rigid principles of orthodox Marxism. They repeated again and again that the coming of socialism is

---

[1] *ibidem*, p. XII.
[2] Marx, *Der Bürgerkrieg in Frankreich,* ed. by Pfemfert (Berlin 1919), *passim.*

Full maturity of Capitalism brings about socialism.

unavoidable. They emphasized the inherent revolutionary character of their parties. Nothing could arouse their anger more than when somebody dared to dispute their adamant revolutionary spirit. However, in fact they were parliamentary parties like all other parties.

From a correct Marxian point of view, as expressed in the later writings of Marx and Engels (but not yet in the Communist Manifesto), all measures designed to restrain, to regulate and to improve capitalism were simply "petty-bourgeois" nonsense stemming from an ignorance of the immanent laws of capitalist evolution. True socialists should not place any obstacles in the way of capitalist evolution. For only the full maturity of capitalism could bring about socialism. It is not only vain, but harmful to the interests of the proletarians to resort to such measures. Even labor-unionism is not an adequate means for the improvement of the conditions of the workers.[1] Marx did not believe that interventionism could benefit the masses. He violently rejected the idea that such measures as minimum wage rates, price ceilings, restriction of interest rates, social security and so on are preliminary steps in bringing about socialism. He aimed at the radical abolition of the wages system which can be accomplished only by communism in its higher phase. He would have sarcastically ridiculed the idea of abolishing the "commodity character" of labor within the frame of a capitalist society by the enactment of a law.

But the socialist parties as they operated in the European countries were virtually no less committed to interventionism than the *Sozialpolitik* of the Kaiser's Germany and the American New Deal. It was against this policy that Georges Sorel and Syndicalism directed their attacks. Sorel, a timid intellectual of a bourgeois background, deprecated the "degeneration" of the socialist parties for which he blamed their penetration by bourgeois intellectuals. He wanted to see the spirit of ruthless aggressiveness, inherent in the masses, revived and freed from the guardianship of intellectual cowards. For Sorel nothing counted but riots. He advocated *action directe,* i.e., sabotage and the general strike as initiatory steps toward the final great revolution.

---

[1] Marx, *Value, Price and Profit,* edited by Eleanor Marx Aveling (New York, 1901), pp. 72-74.

Sorel had success mostly among snobbish and idle intellectuals and no less snobbish and idle heirs of wealthy entrepreneurs. He did not perceptibly move the masses. For the Marxian parties his passionate criticism was hardly more than a nuisance. His historical importance consisted mainly in the role his ideas played in the evolution of Russian Bolshevism and Italian Fascism.

In order to understand the mentality of the Bolshevists we must again refer to the dogmas of Karl Marx. Marx was fully convinced that capitalism is a stage of economic history which is not limited to a few advanced countries only. Capitalism has the tendency to convert all parts of the world into capitalist countries. The bourgeoisie forces all nations to become capitalist nations. When the final hour of capitalism sounds, the whole world will be uniformly in the stage of mature capitalism, ripe for the transition to socialism. Socialism will emerge at the same time in all parts of the world.

Marx erred on this point no less than in all his other statements. Today even the Marxians cannot and do not deny that there still prevail enormous differences in the development of capitalism in various countries. They realize that there are many countries which, from the point of view of the Marxian interpretation of history, must be described as precapitalistic. In these countries the bourgeoisie has not yet attained a ruling position and has not yet set the historical stage of capitalism which is the necessary prerequisite of the appearance of socialism. These countries therefore must first accomplish their "bourgeois revolution" and must go through all phases of capitalism before there can be any question of transforming them into socialist countries. The only policy which Marxians could adopt in such countries would be to support the bourgeois unconditionally, first in their endeavors to seize power and then in their capitalistic ventures. A Marxian party could for a very long time have no other task than to be subservient to bourgeois liberalism. This alone is the mission which historical materialism, if consistently applied, could assign to Russian Marxians. They would be forced to wait quietly until capitalism should have made their nation ripe for socialism.

But the Russian Marxians did not want to wait. They resorted to a new modification of Marxism according to which it was possible for a nation to jump over one of the stages of historical evolution. They shut their eyes to the fact that this new doctrine was not a modification of Marxism, but rather the denial of the last remnant which was left of it. It was an undisguised return to the pre-Marxian and anti-Marxian socialist teachings according to which men are free to adopt socialism at any time if they consider it as a system more beneficial to the commonweal than capitalism. It utterly exploded all the mysticism inwrought into dialectical materialism and in the alleged Marxian discovery of the inexorable laws of mankind's economic evolution.

Having emancipated themselves from Marxian determinism, the Russian Marxians were free to discuss the most appropriate tactics for the realization of socialism in their country. They were no longer bothered with economic problems. They had no longer to investigate whether or not the time had come. They had only one task to accomplish, the seizure of the reins of government.

One group maintained that lasting success could only be expected if the support of a sufficient number of the people, though not necessarily of the majority, could be won. Another group did not favor such a time-consuming procedure. They suggested a bold stroke. A small group of fanatics should be organized as the vanguard of the revolution. Strict discipline and unconditional obedience to the chief should make these professional revolutionists fit for a sudden attack. They should supplant the Czarist government and then rule the country according to the traditional methods of the Czar's police.

The terms used to signify these two groups — Bolshevists (majority) for the latter and Mensheviks (minority) for the former — refer to a vote taken in 1903 at a meeting held for the discussion of these tactical issues. The only difference dividing the two groups from one another was this matter of tactical methods. They both agreed with regard to the ultimate end: socialism.

Both sects tried to justify their respective points of view by quoting passages from Marx's and Engels' writings. This is, of course, the Marxian custom. And each sect was in a position to discover in these sacred books dicta confirming its own stand.

Lenin, the Bolshevist chief, knew his countrymen much better than his adversaries and their leader, Plekhanov, did. He did not, like Plekhanov, make the mistake of applying to Russians the standards of the Western nations. He remembered how twice foreign women had simply usurped supreme power and quietly ruled for a life-time. He was aware of the fact that the terrorist methods of the Czar's secret police were very successful, and he was confident that he could considerably improve on these methods. He was a ruthless dictator and he knew that the Russians lacked the courage to resist oppression. Like Cromwell, Robespierre and Napoleon, he was an ambitious usurper and fully trusted the absence of revolutionary spirit in the immense majority. The autocracy of the Romanovs was doomed because the unfortunate Nicholas II was a weakling. The socialist lawyer Kerensky failed because he was committed to the principle of parliamentary government. Lenin succeeded because he never aimed at anything else than his own dictatorship. And the Russians yearned for a dictator, for a successor of the Terrible Ivan.

The rule of Nicholas II was not ended by a real revolutionary upheaval. It collapsed on the battle fields. Anarchy resulted which Kerensky could not master. A skirmish in the streets of Saint Petersburg removed Kerensky. A short time later Lenin had his 18th Brumaire. In spite of all the terror practised by the Bolshevists the Constituent Assembly, elected by universal franchise for men and women, had only about twenty per cent Bolshevist members. Lenin dispelled by force of arms the Constituent Assembly. The short-lived "liberal" interlude was liquidated. Russia passed from the hands of the inept Romanovs into those of a real autocrat.

Lenin did not content himself with the conquest of Russia. He was fully convinced that he was destined to bring the bliss of socialism to all nations, not only to Russia. The official name which he chose for his government — Union of the Soviet Socialist Republics — does not contain any reference to Russia. It was designed as the nucleus of a world government. It was implied that all foreign comrades by rights owed allegiance to this government and that all foreign bourgeois who dared to resist were guilty of high treason and deserved capital punishment. Lenin did not doubt in the least that all Western countries were on the eve of the great final revolution. He daily expected its outbreak.

40

There was in the opinion of Lenin only one group in Europe that might — although without any prospect of success — try to prevent the revolutionary upheaval: the depraved members of the intelligentsia who had usurped the leadership of the socialist parties. Lenin had long hated these men for their addiction to parliamentary procedure and their reluctance to endorse his dictatorial aspirations. He raged against them because he made them alone responsible for the fact that the socialist parties had supported the war effort of their countries. Already in his Swiss exile, which ended in 1917, Lenin began to split the European socialist parties. Now he set up a new, a Third International which he controlled in the same dictatorial manner in which he directed the Russian Bolshevists. For this new party Lenin chose the name Communist Party. The communists were to fight unto death the various European socialist parties, these "social traitors," and they were to arrange the immediate liquidation of the bourgeoisie and seizure of power by the armed workers. Lenin did not differentiate between socialism and communism as social systems. The goal which he aimed at was not called communism as opposed to socialism. The official name of the Soviet government is Union of the *Socialist* (not of the *Communist*) Soviet Republics. In this regard he did not want to alter the traditional terminology which considered the terms as synonymous. He merely called his partisans, the only sincere and consistent supporters of the revolutionary principles of orthodox Marxism, *communists* and their tactical methods *communism* because he wanted to distinguish them from the "treacherous hirelings of the capitalist exploiters," the wicked Social Democratic leaders like Kautsky and Albert Thomas. These traitors, he emphasized, were anxious to preserve capitalism. They were not true socialists. The only genuine Marxians were those who rejected the name of socialists, irremediably fallen into disrepute.

Thus the distinction between communists and socialists came into being. Those Marxians who did not surrender to the dictator in Moscow called themselves social democrats or, in short, socialists. What characterized them was the belief that the most appropriate method for the realization of their plans to establish socialism, the final goal common to them as well as to the communists, was to win the support of the majority of their fellow-citizens. They abandoned the revolutionary slogans and tried to adopt democratic methods for the seizure of power. They did not bother about the problem whether or not a socialist regime is compatible with democracy. But for the attainment of socialism they were resolved to apply democratic procedures only.

The communists, on the other hand, were in the early years of the Third International firmly committed to the principle of revolution and civil war. They were loyal only to their Russian chief. They expelled from their ranks everybody who was suspected of feeling himself bound by any of his country's laws. They plotted unceasingly and squandered blood in unsuccessful riots.

Lenin could not understand why the communists failed everywhere outside Russia. He did not expect much from the American workers. In the United States, the communists agreed, the workers lacked the revolutionary spirit because they were spoiled by well-being and steeped in the vice of money-making. But Lenin did not doubt that the European masses were class-conscious and therefore fully committed to revolutionary ideas. The only reason why the revolution had not been realized was in his opinion the inadequacy and cowardice of the communist officials. Again and again he deposed his vicars and appointed new men. But he did not succeed any better.

Slowly the communists in the democratic countries "degenerated" into parliamentary parties. Like the old socialist parties before 1914, they continue to pay lip service to the revolutionary ideas. But the revolutionary spirit is more powerful in the parlour-rooms of the heirs of millionaires than in the modest homes of the workers. In the Anglo-Saxon and in the Latin-American countries the socialist voters place confidence in democratic methods. Here the number of people who seriously aim at a communist revolution is very small. Most of those who publicly proclaim their adherence to the principles of communism would feel extremely unhappy if the revolution were to arise and expose their lives and their property to danger. If the Russian armies were to march into their countries or if domestic communists were to seize power without engaging them in the fight, they would probably rejoice in the hope of being rewarded for their Marxian orthodoxy. But they themselves do not long for revolutionary laurels.

It is a fact that in all these thirty years of passionate pro-Soviet agitation not a single country outside Russia went communist of its citizens' own accord. Eastern Europe turned to communism only when the diplomatic arrangements of international power politics had converted it into a sphere of exclusive Russian influence and hegemony. It is very unlikely that Western Germany, France, Italy and Spain will espouse communism if the United States and Great Britain do not adopt a policy of absolute diplomatic *"désintéressement."* What gives strength to the communist movement in these and in some other countries is the belief that Russia is driven by an unflinching "dynamism" while the Anglo-Saxon powers are indifferent and not very much interested in their fate.

Marx and the Marxians erred lamentably when they assumed that the masses long for a revolutionary overthrow of the "bourgeois" order of society. The militant communists are to be found only in the ranks of those who make a living from their communism or expect that a revolution would further their personal ambitions. The subversive activities of these professional plotters are dangerous precisely on account of the naivete of those who are merely flirting with the revolutionary idea. Those confused and misguided sympathizers who call themselves "liberals" and whom the communists call "useful innocents," the fellow-travellers and even the majority of the officially registered party members, would be terribly frightened if they were to discover one day that their chiefs mean business when preaching sedition. But then it may be too late to avert disaster.

For the time being, the ominous peril of the communist parties in the West lies in their stand on foreign affairs. The distinctive mark of all present-day communist parties is their devotion to the aggressive foreign policy of the Soviets. Whenever they must choose between Russia and their own country, they do not hesitate to prefer Russia. Their principle is: Right or wrong, my Russia. They strictly obey all orders issued from Moscow. When Russia was an ally of Hitler, the French communists sabotaged their own country's war effort and the American communists passionately opposed President Roosevelt's plans to aid the democracies in their struggle against the Nazis. The communists all over the world branded all those who defended themselves against the German invaders as "imperialist warmongers." But as soon as Hitler attacked Russia, the imperialist war of the capitalists over night changed into a just war of defense. Whenever Stalin conquers one more country, the communists justify this aggression as an act of self-defense against "Fascists."

In their blind worship of everything that is Russian, the communists of Western Europe and the United States by far surpass the worst excesses ever committed by chauvinists. They wax rapturous about Russian movies, Russian music and the alleged discoveries of Russian science. They speak in ecstatic words about the economic achievements of the Soviets. They ascribe the victory of the United Nations to the deeds of the Russian armed forces. Russia, they contend, has saved the world from the Fascist menace. Russia is the only free country while all other nations are subject to the dictatorship of the capitalists. The Russians alone are happy and enjoy the bliss of living a full life; in the capitalist countries the immense majority are suffering from frustration and unfulfilled desires. Just as the pious Muslim yearns for a pilgrimage to the Prophet's tomb at Mecca, so the communist intellectual deems a pilgrimage to the holy shrines of Moscow as the event of his life.

However, the distinction in the use of the terms communists and socialists did not affect the meaning of the terms communism and socialism as applied to the final goal of the policies common to them both. It was only in 1928, that the program of the Communist International, adopted by the sixth congress in Moscow,[1] began to differentiate between communism and socialism (and not merely between communists and socialists).

According to this new doctrine there is, in the economic evolution of mankind, between the historical stage of capitalism and that of communism a third stage, namely that of socialism. Socialism is a social system based on public control of the means of production and full management of all processes of production and distribution by a planning central authority. In this regard it is equal to communism. But it differs from communism insofar as there is no equality of the portions allotted to each individual for his own consumption. There are still wages paid to the comrades, and these

---

[1] Cf. *Blueprint for World Conquest as Outlined by the Communist International,* Human Events (Washington and Chicago), 1946, pp. 181-182.

wage rates are graduated according to economic expediency as far as the central authority deems it necessary for securing the greatest possible output of products. What Stalin calls socialism corresponds by and large to Marx's concept of the "early phase" of communism. Stalin reserves the term communism exclusively to what Marx called the "higher phase" of communism. Socialism, in the sense in which Stalin has lately used the term, is moving toward communism, but is in itself not yet communism. Socialism will turn into communism as soon as the increase in wealth to be expected from the operation of the socialist methods of production has raised the lower standard of living of the Russian masses to the higher standard which the distinguished holders of important offices enjoy in present-day Russia.[1]

The apologetical character of this new terminological practice is obvious. Stalin finds it necessary to explain to the vast majority of his subjects why their standard of living is extremely low, much lower than that of the masses in the capitalist countries and even lower than that of the Russian proletarians in the days of Czarist rule. He wants to justify the fact that salaries and wages are unequal, that a small group of Soviet officials enjoys all the luxuries modern technique can provide, that a second group, more numerous than the first one, but less numerous than the middle class in imperial Russia, lives in "bourgeois" style, while the masses, ragged and barefooted, subsist in congested slums and are poorly fed. He can no longer blame capitalism for this state of affairs. Thus he was compelled to resort to a new ideological makeshift.

Stalin's problem was the more burning as the Russian communists in the early days of their rule had passionately proclaimed income equality as a principle to be enforced from the first instant of the proletarians' seizure of power. Moreover, in the capitalist countries the most powerful demagogic trick applied by the Russia-sponsored communist parties is to excite the envy of those with lower incomes against all those with higher incomes. The main argument advanced by the communists for the support of their thesis that Hitler's National Socialism was not genuine socialism, but, on the contrary, the worst variety of capitalism, was that there was in Nazi Germany inequality in the standard of living.

---

[1] Cf. David J. Dallin, *The Real Soviet Russia* (Yale University Press 1944), pp. 88-95.

Stalin's new distinction between socialism and communism is in open contradiction to the policy of Lenin and no less to the tenets of the propaganda of the communist parties outside the Russian frontiers. But such contradictions do not matter in the realm of the Soviets. The word of the dictator is the ultimate decision, and nobody is so foolhardy as to venture opposition.

It is important to realize that Stalin's semantical innovation affects merely the terms communism and socialism. He did not alter the meaning of the terms socialist and communist. The Bolshevist party is just as before called communist. The Russophile parties beyond the borders of the Soviet Union call themselves communist parties and are violently fighting the socialist parties which in their eyes are simply social traitors. But the official name of the Union of Soviet *Socialist* Republics remains unchanged.

4

Russia's Aggressiveness

THE German, Italian and Japanese nationalists justified their aggressive policies by their lack of *Lebensraum*. Their countries are comparatively overpopulated. They are poorly endowed by nature and depend on the import of foodstuffs and raw materials from abroad. They must export manufactures to pay for these badly needed imports. But the protectionist policies espoused by the countries producing a surplus of foodstuffs and raw materials close their frontiers to import of manufactures. The world is manifestly tending toward a state of full economic autarchy of each nation. In such a world, what fate is in store for those nations who can neither feed nor clothe their citizens out of domestic resources?

The *Lebensraum* doctrine of the self-styled "have-not" peoples emphasizes that there are in America and in Australia millions of acres of unused land much more fertile than the barren soil which the farmers of the have-not nations are tilling. Natural conditions for mining and manufacturing are likewise much more propitious than in the countries of the have-nots. But the German, Italian and Japanese peasants and workers are barred from access to these areas favored by nature. The immigration laws of the comparatively underpopulated countries prevent their migration. These laws raise the marginal productivity of labor and thereby wage rates in the underpopulated countries and lower them in the overpopulated countries. The high standard of living in the United States and the British Dominions is paid for by a lowering of the standard of living in the congested countries of Europe and Asia.

The true aggressors, say these German, Italian and Japanese nationalists, are those nations who by means of trade and migration barriers have arrogated to themselves the lion's share of the natural riches of the earth. Has not the Pope himself declared that the root causes of the World Wars are "that cold and calculating egoism which tends to hoard the economic resources and materials destined for the use of all to such an extent that the nations less favored by nature are not permitted access to them?"[1] The war that Hitler, Mussolini and Hirohito kindled was from this point of view a just war, for its only aim was to give to the have-nots what, by virtue of natural and divine right, belongs to them.

The Russians cannot venture to justify their aggressive policy by such arguments. Russia is a comparatively underpopulated country. Its soil is much better endowed by nature than that of any other nation. It offers the most advantageous conditions for the growing of all kinds of cereals, fruits, seeds and plants. Russia owns immense pastures and almost inexhaustible forests. It has the richest resources for the production of gold, silver, platinum, iron, copper, nickel, manganese and all other metals and of oil. But for the despotism of the Czars and the lamentable inadequacy of the communist system its population could long since have enjoyed the highest standard of living. It is certainly not lack of natural resources that pushes Russia toward conquest.

Lenin's aggressiveness was an outgrowth of his conviction that he was the leader of the final world revolution. He considered himself as the legitimate successor of the First International, destined to accomplish the task in which Marx and Engels had failed. He did not believe that any action on his part was required to accelerate the outbreak of the revolution. The knell of capitalism had sounded, and no capitalist machinations could delay the expropriation of the expropriators any longer. What was needed was only the dictator of the new social order. Lenin was ready to take the burden upon his shoulders.

Since the days of the Mongol invasions mankind has not had to face such an unflinching and thorough-going aspiration for unlimited world supremacy. In every country the Russian emissaries and the communist fifth columns were fanatically working for the "Anschluss" to Russia. But Lenin lacked the first four columns. Russia's military forces were at that time contemptible. When they

---

[1] *Christmas Eve Broadcast*, New York Times, December 25, 1941.

crossed the Russian borders, they were stopped by the Poles. They could not march farther West. The great campaign for world conquest petered out.

It was just idle talk to discuss the problems whether communism in one country only is possible or desirable. The communists had failed utterly outside the Russian frontiers. They were forced to stay at home.

Stalin devoted all his energy to the organization of a standing army of a size the world had never seen before. But he was not more successful than Lenin and Trotsky had been. The Nazis easily defeated this army and occupied the most important part of Russia's territory. Russia was saved by the British and, above all, by the American forces. American lend-lease enabled the Russians to follow on the heels of the Germans when the scarcity of equipment and the threatening American invasion forced them to withdraw from Russia. They could even occasionally defeat the rear-guards of the retreating Nazis. They could conquer Berlin and Vienna when the American airplanes had crushed the German defenses. When the Americans had crushed the Japanese, the Russians could quietly stab them in the back.

Of course, the communists inside and outside of Russia and the fellow-travellers passionately contend that it was Russia that defeated the Nazis and liberated Europe. They pass over in silence the fact that the only reason why the Nazis could not crush the defenders of Stalingrad was their lack of munitions, airplanes and gasoline. It was the blockade that made it impossible for the Nazis to provide their armies with the equipment needed and to construct in the occupied Russian territory a transport system that could ship this equipment to the far distant front line. The decisive battle of the war was the battle of the Atlantic. The great strategical events in the war against Germany were the conquest of Africa and Sicily and the victory in Normandy. Stalingrad was, when measured by the gigantic standards of this war, hardly more than a tactical success. In the struggle against the Italians and the Japanese, Russia's share was nil.

But the spoils of the victory go to Russia alone. While the other United Nations do not seek for territorial aggrandizement, the Russians are in full swing. They have annexed the three Baltic

Republics, Bessarabia, Czechoslovakia's province of Carpatho-Russia[1], a part of Finland, a great part of Poland, and huge territories in the far East. They claim the rest of Poland, Rumania, Hungary, Yugoslavia, Bulgaria, Korea and China as their exclusive sphere of influence. They are anxious to establish in these countries "friendly" governments, i.e., puppet governments. But for the opposition raised by the United States and Great Britain they would rule today in the whole of continental Europe, continental Asia and Northern Africa. Only the American and British garrisons in Germany bar the Russians' way to the shores of the Atlantic.

Today, no less than after the first World War, the real menace for the West does not lie in the military power of Russia. Great Britain could easily repel a Russian attack, and it would be sheer lunacy for the Russians to undertake a war against the United States. Not the Russian armies, but the communist ideologies threaten the West. The Russians know it very well and place confidence not in their own army, but in their foreign partisans. They want to overthrow the democracies from within, not from without. Their main weapon is the pro-Russian machinations of their Fifth Columns. These are the crack divisions of Bolshevism.

The communist writers and politicians inside and outside of Russia explain Russia's aggressive policies as mere self-defense. It is, they say, not Russia that plans aggression but, on the contrary, the decaying capitalist democracies. Russia wants merely to defend its own independence. This is an old and well-tried method of justifying aggression. Louis XIV and Napoleon I, Wilhelm II and Hitler were the most peace-loving of all men. When they invaded foreign countries, they did so only in just self-defense. Russia was as much menaced by Esthonia or Latvia as Germany was by Luxemburg or Denmark.

An outgrowth of this fable of self-defense is the legend of the *cordon sanitaire*. The political independence of the small neighbor countries of Russia, it is maintained, is merely a capitalist make-shift designed to prevent the European democracies from being infected with the germ of communism. Hence, it is concluded,

---

[1] The annexation of Carpatho-Russia utterly explodes their hypocritical indignation about the Munich agreements of 1938.

these small nations have forfeited their right to independence. For Russia has the inalienable right to claim that its neighbors — and likewise its neighbors' neighbors — should only be ruled by "friendly," i.e., strictly communist governments. What would happen to the world if all great powers were to make the same pretension?

The truth is that it is not the governments of the democratic nations that aim at overthrowing the present Russian system. They do not foster pro-democratic fifth columns in Russia and they do not incite the Russian masses against their rulers. But the Russians are busy day and night fomenting unrest in every country. Their Third International openly tried to kindle communist revolutions all over the world.

The very lame and hesitant intervention of the Allied Nations in the Russian Civil War was not a pro-capitalist and anti-communist venture. For the Allied Nations, involved in their struggle for life and death with the Germans, Lenin was at that time merely a tool of their deadly foes. Ludendorff had dispatched Lenin to Russia in order to overthrow the Kerensky regime and to bring about the defection of Russia. The Bolshevists fought by force of arms all those Russians who wanted to continue the alliance with France, Great Britain, the United States and the other democratic nations. From a military point of view it was impossible for the Western nations to stay neutral while their Russian allies were desperately defending themselves against the Bolshevists. For the Allied Nations the Eastern Front was at stake. The cause of the "White" generals was their own cause.

As soon as the war against Germany came to an end in 1918, the Allies lost all interest in Russian affairs. There was no longer any need for an Eastern Front. They did not care a whit about the internal problems of Russia. They longed for peace and were anxious to withdraw from the fighting. They were, of course, embarrassed because they did not know how to liquidate their venture with propriety. Their generals were ashamed of abandoning companions in arms who had fought to the best of their abilities in a common cause. To leave these men in the lurch was in their opinion nothing short of cowardice and desertion. Such considerations of military honor delayed for some time the withdrawal of the incon-

51

spicuous Allied detachments and the termination of supplies to the Whites. When this was finally accomplished, the Allied statesmen felt relief. From then on they adopted a policy of strict neutrality with regard to Russian affairs.

It was very unfortunate indeed that the Allied Nations had been willy nilly entangled in the Russian Civil War. It would have been better if the military situation of 1917 and 1918 had not compelled them to interfere. But one must not overlook the fact that the abandonment of intervention in Russia was tantamount to the final failure of President Wilson's policy. The United States had entered the war in order to make "the world safe for democracy." The victory had crushed the Kaiser and substituted in Germany a republican government for the comparatively mild and limited imperial autocracy. On the other hand, it had resulted in Russia in establishing a dictatorship compared with which the despotism of the Czars could be called liberal. But the Allies were not eager to make Russia safe for democracy as they had tried to do with Germany. After all the Kaiser's Germany had parliaments, ministers responsible to the parliaments, trial by jury, freedom of thought, of religion and of the press not much more limited than in the West, and many other democratic institutions. But Soviet Russia was an unlimited despotism.

The Americans, the French and the British failed to see things from this angle. But the antidemocratic forces in Germany, Italy, Poland, Hungary and the Balkans thought differently. As the nationalists of these countries interpreted it, the neutrality of the Allied Powers with regard to Russia was evidence of the fact that their concern for democracy had been a mere blind. The Allies, they argued, had fought Germany because they envied Germany's economic prosperity, and they spared the new Russian autocracy because they were not afraid of Russian economic power. Democracy, these nationalists concluded, was nothing else than a convenient catchword to delude gullible people. And they became frightened that the emotional appeal of this slogan would one day be used as a disguise for insidious assaults against their own independence.

Since the abandonment of the intervention Russia had certainly no longer any reason to fear the great Western powers. Neither were the Soviets afraid of a Nazi aggression. The assertions to the contrary, very popular in Western Europe and in America, resulted from complete ignorance of German affairs. But the Russians knew Germany and the Nazis. They had read *Mein Kampf.* They learned from this book not only that Hitler coveted the Ukraine, but also that Hitler's fundamental strategical idea was to embark upon the conquest of Russia only after having definitely and forever annihilated France. The Russians were fully convinced that Hitler's expectation, as expressed in *Mein Kampf,* that Great Britain and the United States would keep out of this war and would quietly let France be destroyed, was vain. They were certain that such a new world war, in which they themselves planned to stay neutral, would result in a new German defeat. And this defeat, they argued, would make Germany — if not the whole of Europe — safe for Bolshevism. Guided by this opinion Stalin already in the time of the Weimar Republic aided the then secret German rearmament. The German communists helped the Nazis as much as they could in their endeavors to undermine the Weimar regime. Finally Stalin entered in August 1939 into an open alliance with Hitler, in order to give him a free hand against the West.

What Stalin — like all other people — did not anticipate was the overwhelming success of the German armies in 1940. Hitler attacked Russia in 1941 because he was fully convinced that not only France but also Great Britain were done for and that the United States, menaced in the rear by Japan, would not be strong enough to interfere successfully with European affairs.

The disintegration of the Hapsburg Empire in 1918 and the Nazi defeat in 1945 have opened the gates of Europe to Russia. Russia is today the only military power on the European continent. But why are the Russians so intent upon conquering and annexing? They certainly do not need the resources of these countries. Neither is Stalin driven by the idea that such conquests could increase his popularity with the Russian masses. His subjects are indifferent to military glory.

It is not the masses whom Stalin wants to placate by his aggressive policy, but the intellectuals. For their Marxian orthodoxy is at stake, the very foundation of the Soviet might.

These Russian intellectuals were narrow-minded enough to ab-

53

sorb modifications of the Marxian creed which were in fact an abandonment of the essential teachings of dialectical materialism, provided that these modifications flattered their Russian chauvinism. They swallowed the doctrine that their holy Russia could jump over one of the inextricable stages of economic evolution as described by Marx. They prided themselves on being the vanguard of the proletariat and the world revolution who, by realizing socialism first in one country only, set up a glorious example for all other nations. But it is impossible to explain to them why the other nations do not finally catch up with Russia. In the writings of Marx and Engels, which one cannot keep out of their hands, they discover that the fathers of Marxism considered Great Britain and France, and even Germany, as the countries most advanced in civilization and in the evolution of capitalism. These students of the Marxian universities may be too dull to comprehend the philosophical and economic doctrines of the Marxian gospel. But they are not too dull to see that Marx considered those Western countries as much more advanced than Russia.

Then some of these students of economic policies and statistics begin to suspect that the standard of living of the masses is much higher in the capitalist countries than in their own country. How can this be? Why are conditions much more propitious in the United States which — although foremost in capitalist production — is most backward in awakening class-consciousness in the proletarians?

The inference from these facts seems inescapable. If the most advanced countries do not adopt communism and fare rather well under capitalism, if communism is limited to a country which Marx considered as backward and does not bring about riches for all, is not perhaps the correct interpretation that communism is a feature of backward countries and results in general poverty? Must not a Russian patriot be ashamed of the fact that his country is committed to this system?

Such thoughts are very dangerous in a despotic country. Whoever dared to express them, would be mercilessly liquidated by the G.P.U. But even unspoken, they are on the tip of every intelligent man's tongue. They trouble the sleep of the supreme officials and perhaps even that of the great dictator. He certainly has the power

54

to crush every opponent. But considerations of expediency make it inadvisable to eradicate all somewhat judicious people and to run the country only with stupid blockheads.

This is the real crisis of Russian Marxism. Every day that passes without bringing the world revolution aggravates it. The Soviets must conquer the world or else they are menaced in their own country by a defection of the intelligentsia. It is concern about the ideological state of Russia's shrewdest minds that pushes Stalin's Russia toward unflinching aggression.

5

Trotsky's Heresy

THE dictatorial doctrine as accepted by the Russian Bolshevists, the Italian Fascists and the German Nazis tacitly implies that there cannot arise any disagreement with regard to the question who shall be the dictator. The mystical forces directing the course of historical events designate the providential leader. All righteous people are bound to submit to the unfathomable decrees of history and to bend their knees before the throne of the man of destiny. Those who decline to do so are heretics, abject scoundrels who must be "liquidated."

In reality the dictatorial power is seized by that candidate who succeeds in exterminating in time all his rivals and their helpers. The dictator paves his way to supreme power by slaughtering all his competitors. He preserves his eminent position by butchering all those who could possibly dispute it. The history of all oriental despotisms bears witness to this, as well as the experience of contemporary dictatorship.

When Lenin died in 1924, Stalin supplanted his most dangerous rival Trotsky. Trotsky escaped, spent years abroad in various countries of Europe, Asia and America and was finally assassinated in Mexico City. Stalin became the absolute ruler of Russia.

Trotsky was an intellectual of the orthodox Marxian type. As such he tried to represent his personal feud with Stalin as a conflict of principles. He tried to construct a Trotsky doctrine as distinguished from the Stalin doctrine. He branded Stalin's policies as an apostasy from the sacred legacy of Marx and Lenin. Stalin retorted in the same way. In fact, however, the conflict was a rivalry of two men, not a conflict of antagonistic ideas and principles. There was some minor dissent with regard to tactical methods.

But in all essential matters Stalin and Trotsky were in agreement.

Trotsky had lived, before 1917, many years in foreign countries and was to some degree familiar with the main languages of the Western peoples. He posed as an expert in international affairs. Actually he did not know anything about Western civilization, political ideas and economic conditions. As a wandering exile he had moved almost exclusively in the circles of his fellow-exiles. The only foreigners whom he had met occasionally in coffee-houses and club-rooms of Western and Central Europe were radical doctrinaires, by their Marxian prepossessions precluded from reality. His main reading was Marxian books and periodicals. He scorned all other writings as "bourgeois" literature. He was absolutely unfitted to see events from any other angle than that of Marxism. Like Marx he was ready to interpret every great strike and every small riot as the sign of the outbreak of the final great revolution.

Stalin is a poorly educated Georgian. He has not the slightest knowledge of any Western language. He does not know Europe or America. Even his achievements as a Marxian author are questionable. But it was precisely the fact that, although an adamant supporter of communism, he was not indoctrinated with Marxian dogmas that made him superior to Trotsky. Stalin could see things as they really were without being deluded by the spurious tenets of dialectical materialism. When faced with a problem, he'did not search for an interpretation in the writings of Marx and Engels. He trusted his common-sense. He was judicious enough to discern the fact that the policy of world revolution as inaugurated by Lenin and Trotsky in 1917 had failed completely outside the borders of Russia.

In Germany the communists, led by Karl Liebknecht and Rosa Luxemburg, were crushed by detachments of the regular army and by nationalist volunteers in a bloody battle fought in January, 1919, in the streets of Berlin. The communist seizure of power in Munich in spring, 1919, and the Hölz riot in March, 1921, ended likewise in disaster. In Hungary, in 1919, the communists were defeated by Horthy and Gömbös and the Rumanian army. In Austria various communist plots failed in 1918 and 1919; a violent upheaval in July, 1927, was easily quelled by the Vienna police. In Italy, in 1920, the occupation of the factories was a complete miscarriage. In France and in Switzerland the communist propaganda seemed to be very powerful in the first years following the Armistice of 1918; but it evaporated very soon. In Great Britain, in 1926, the general strike called by the labor unions resulted in lamentable failure.

Trotsky was so blinded by his orthodoxy that he refused to admit that the Bolshevist methods had failed. But Stalin realized it very well. He did not abandon the idea of instigating revolutionary outbreaks in all foreign countries and of conquering the whole world for the Soviets. But he was fully aware of the fact that it was necessary to postpone the aggression for a few years and to resort to new methods for its execution. Trotsky was wrong in accusing Stalin of strangling the communist movement outside of Russia. What Stalin really did was to apply other means for the attainment of ends which are common to him and all other Marxians.

As an exegetic of Marxian dogmas Stalin was certainly inferior to Trotsky. But he surpassed his rival by far as a politician. Bolshevism owes its tactical successes in world policies to Stalin, not to Trotsky.

In the field of domestic policies, Trotsky resorted to the well-tried traditional tricks which Marxians had always applied in criticizing socialist measures adopted by other parties. Whatever Stalin did was not true socialism and communism, but, on the contrary, the very opposite of it, a monstrous perversion of the lofty principles of Marx and Lenin. All the disastrous features of public control of production and distribution as they appeared in Russia were, in Trotsky's interpretation, brought about by Stalin's petty-bourgeois policies. They were not unavoidable consequences of communist methods. They were attendant phenomena of Stalinism, not of communism. It was exclusively Stalin's fault that an absolutist irresponsible bureaucracy was supreme, that a class of privileged oligarchs enjoyed luxuries while the masses lived on the verge of starvation, that a terrorist regime executed the old guard of revolutionaries and condemned millions to slave labor in concentration camps, that the secret police was omnipotent, that the labor unions were powerless, that the masses were deprived of all rights and liberties. Stalin was not a champion of the egalitarian classless society. He was the pioneer of a return to the worst methods of class rule and exploitation. A new ruling class of about 10% of the population ruthlessly oppressed and exploited the immense majority of toiling proletarians.

Trotsky was at a loss to explain how all this could be achieved by only one man and his few sycophants. Where were the "material productive forces," much talked about in Marxian historical materialism, which — "independent of the wills of individuals" — determine the course of human events "with the inexorability of a law of nature?" How could it happen that one man was in a position to alter the "juridical and political superstructure" which is uniquely and inalterably fixed by the economic structure of society? Even Trotsky agreed that there was no longer any private ownership of the means of production in Russia. In Stalin's empire, production and distribution are entirely controlled by "society." It is a fundamental dogma of Marxism that the superstructure of such a system must necessarily be the bliss of the earthly paradise. There is in Marxian doctrines no room for an interpretation blaming individuals for a degenerative process which could convert the blessing of public control of business into evil. A consistent Marxian — if consistency were compatible with Marxism — would have to admit that Stalin's political system was the necessary superstructure of communism.

All essential items in Trotsky's program were in perfect agreement with the policies of Stalin. Trotsky advocated the industrialization of Russia. It was this that Stalin's Five-Year Plan aimed at. Trotsky advocated the collectivization of agriculture. Stalin established the Kolkhoz and liquidated the Kulaks. Trotsky favored the organization of a big army. Stalin organized such an army. Neither was Trotsky when still in power a friend of democracy. He was, on the contrary, a fanatical supporter of dictatorial oppression of all "saboteurs." It is true, he did not anticipate that the dictator could consider him, Trotsky, author of Marxian tracts and veteran of the glorious extermination of the Romanovs, as the most wicked saboteur. Like all other advocates of dictatorship, he assumed that he himself or one of his intimate friends would be the dictator.

Trotsky was a critic of bureaucratism. But he did not suggest any other method for the conduct of affairs in a socialist system.

There is no other alternative to profit-seeking private business than bureaucratic management.[1]

The truth is that Trotsky found only one fault with Stalin: that he, Stalin, was the dictator and not himself, Trotsky. In their feud they both were right. Stalin was right in maintaining that his regime was the embodiment of communist principles. Trotsky was right in asserting that Stalin's regime had made Russia a hell.

Trotskyism did not entirely disappear with Trotsky's death. Boulangerism in France, too, survived for some time the end of General Boulanger. There are still Carlists left in Spain although the line of Don Carlos died out. Such posthumous movements are, of course, doomed.

But in all countries there are people who, although themselves fanatically committed to the idea of all-round planning, i.e., public ownership of the means of production, become frightened when they are confronted with the real face of communism. These people are disappointed. They dream of a Garden of Eden. For them communism, or socialism, means an easy life in riches and the full enjoyment of all liberties and pleasures. They fail to realize the contradictions inherent in their image of the communist society. They have uncritically swallowed all the lunatic fantasies of Charles Fourier and all the absurdities of Veblen. They firmly believe in Engels' assertion that socialism will be a realm of unlimited freedom. They indict capitalism for every thing they dislike and are fully convinced that socialism will deliver them from all evil. They ascribe their own failures and frustrations to the unfairness of this "mad" competitive system and expect that socialism will assign them that eminent position and high income which by right are due to them. They are Cinderellas yearning for the prince-savior who will recognize their merits and virtues. The loathing of capitalism and the worship of communism are consolations for them. They help them to disguise to themselves their own inferiority and to blame the "system" for their own shortcomings.

In advocating dictatorship such people always advocate the dictatorship of their own clique. In asking for planning, what they have in mind is always their own plan, not that of others. They will never admit that a socialist or communist regime is true and

---

[1] Cf. Mises, *Bureaucracy* (Yale University Press, 1944).

genuine socialism or communism, if it does not assign to themselves the most eminent position and the highest income. For them the essential feature of true and genuine communism is that all affairs are precisely conducted according to their own will and that all those who disagree are beaten into submission.

It is a fact that the majority of our contemporaries are imbued with socialist and communist ideas. However, this does not mean that they are unanimous in their proposals for socialization of the means of production and public control of production and distribution. On the contrary. Each socialist coterie is fanatically opposed to the plans of all other socialist groups. The various socialist sects fight one another most bitterly.

If the case of Trotsky — and the analogous case of Gregor Strasser in Nazi Germany — were isolated cases, there would be no need to deal with them. But they are not casual incidents. They are typical. Study of them reveals the psychological causes both of the popularity of socialism and of its unfeasibility.

6

The Liberation of the Demons

THE history of mankind is the history of ideas. For it is ideas, theories, and doctrines that guide human action, determine the ultimate ends men aim at and the choice of the means employed for the attainment of these ends. The sensational events which stir the emotions and catch the interest of superficial observers are merely the consummation of ideological changes. There are no such things as abrupt sweeping transformations of human affairs. What is called, in rather misleading terms, a "turning point in history" is the coming on the scene of forces which were already for a long time at work behind the scene. New ideologies, which had already long since superseded the old ones, throw off their last veil, and even the dullest people become aware of the changes which they did not notice before.

In this sense Lenin's seizure of power in October 1917, was certainly a turning point. But its meaning was very different from that which the communists attribute to it.

The Soviet victory played only a minor role in the evolution toward socialism. The pro-socialist policies of the industrial countries of Central and Western Europe were of much greater consequence in this regard. Bismarck's social security scheme was a more momentous pioneering on the way toward socialism than was the expropriation of the backward Russian manufactures. The Prussian National Railways had provided the only instance of a government-operated business which, for some time at least, had avoided manifest financial failure. The British had already before 1914 adopted essential parts of the German social security system. In all industrial countries, the governments were committed to interventionist policies which were bound to result ultimately in socialism. During the war most of them embarked upon what was called war socialism. The German Hindenburg Program which, of course, could not be executed completely on account of Germany's defeat, was no less radical but much better designed than the much talked-about Russian Five-Year Plans.

For the socialists in the predominantly industrial countries of the West, the Russian methods could not be of any use. For these countries, production of manufactures for export was indispensable. They could not adopt the Russian system of economic autarky. Russia had never exported manufactures in quantities worth mentioning. Under the Soviet system it withdrew almost entirely from the world market of cereals and raw materials. Even fanatical socialists could not help admitting that the West could not learn anything from Russia. It is obvious that the technological achievements in which the Bolshevist gloried were merely clumsy imitations of things accomplished in the West. Lenin defined communism as: "the Soviet power plus electrification." Now, electrification was certainly not of Russian origin, and the Western nations surpass Russia in the field of electrification no less than in every other branch of industry.

The real significance of the Lenin revolution is to be seen in the fact that it was the bursting forth of the principle of unrestricted violence and oppression. It was the negation of all the political ideals that had for three thousand years guided the evolution of Western civilization.

State and government are nothing else than the social apparatus of violent coercion and repression. Such an apparatus, the police power, is indispensable in order to prevent antisocial individuals and bands from destroying social cooperation. Violent prevention and suppression of antisocial activities benefit the whole of society and each of its members. But violence and oppression are nonetheless evils and corrupt those in charge of their application. It is necessary to restrict the power of those in office lest they become absolute despots. Society cannot exist without an apparatus of violent coercion. But neither can it exist if the office holders are irresponsible tyrants free to inflict harm upon those they dislike.

It is the social function of the laws to curb the arbitrariness of

63

the police. The rule of law restricts the arbitrariness of the officers as much as possible. It strictly limits their discretion and thus assigns to the citizens a sphere in which they are free to act without being frustrated by government interference.

Freedom and liberty always mean freedom from police interference. In nature there are no such things as liberty and freedom. There is only the adamant rigidity of the laws of nature to which man must unconditionally submit if he wants to attain any ends at all. Neither was there liberty in the imaginary paradisaical conditions which according to the fantastic prattle of many writers preceded the establishment of societal bonds. Where there is no government, everybody is at the mercy of his stronger neighbor. Liberty can be realized only within an established state ready to prevent a gangster from killing and robbing his weaker fellows. But it is the rule of law alone which hinders the rulers from turning themselves into the worst gangsters.

The laws establish norms of legitimate action. They fix the procedures required for the repeal or alteration of existing laws and for the enactment of new laws. They likewise fix the procedures required for the application of the laws in definite cases, the due process of law. They establish courts and tribunals. Thus they are intent upon avoiding a situation in which the individuals are at the mercy of the rulers.

Mortal men are liable to error, and legislators and judges are mortal men. It may happen again and again that the valid laws or their interpretation by the courts prevent the executive organs from resorting to some measures which could be beneficial. No great harm, however, can result. If the legislators recognize the deficiency of the valid laws, they can alter them. It is certainly a bad thing that a criminal may sometimes evade punishment because there is a loophole left in the law or because the prosecutor has neglected some formalities. But it is the minor evil when compared with the consequences of unlimited discretionary power on the part of the "benevolent" despot.

It is precisely this point which antisocial individuals fail to see. Such people condemn the formalism of the due process of law. Why should the laws hinder the government from resorting to beneficial measures? Is it not fetishism to make the laws supreme

64

and not expediency? They advocate the substitution of the welfare state (*Wohlfahrtsstaat*) for the state governed by the rule of law (*Rechtsstaat*). In this welfare state, paternal government should be free to accomplish all things it considers beneficial to the common-weal. No "scraps of paper" should restrain an enlightened ruler in his endeavors to promote the general welfare. All opponents must be crushed mercilessly lest they frustrate the beneficial action of the government. No empty formalities must protect them any longer against their well-deserved punishment.

It is customary to call the point of view of the advocates of the welfare state the "social" point of view as distinguished from the "individualistic" and "selfish" point of view of the champions of the rule of law. In fact, however, the supporters of the welfare state are utterly antisocial and intolerant zealots. For their ideology tacitly implies that the government will exactly execute what they themselves deem as right and beneficial. They entirely disregard the possibility that there could arise disagreement with regard to the question of what is right and expedient and what is not. They advocate enlightened despotism, but they are convinced that the enlightened despot will in every detail comply with their own opinion concerning the measures to be adopted. They favor planning, but what they have in mind is exclusively their own plan, not those of their citizens. They want to exterminate all opponents, that is, all those who disagree with them. They are utterly intolerant and are not prepared to allow any dissension. Every advocate of the welfare state and of planning is a potential dictator. What he plans is to deprive all other men of all their rights and to establish his own and his friends' unrestricted omnipotence. He refuses to convince his fellow-citizens. He prefers to "liquidate" them. He scorns the "bourgeois" society that worships law and legal procedure. He himself worships violence and bloodshed.

The irreconcilable conflict of these two doctrines, rule of law versus welfare state, was at issue in all the struggles which men fought for liberty. It was a long and hard evolution. Again and again the champions of absolutism triumphed. But finally the rule of law predominated in the realm of Western civilization. The rule of law, or limited government, as safeguarded by constitutions and bills of rights, is the characteristic mark of this civilization.

It was the rule of law that brought about the marvelous achievements of modern capitalism and of its — as consistent Marxians should say — "superstructure," democracy. It secured for a steadily increasing population unprecedented well-being. The masses in the capitalist countries enjoy today a standard of living far above that of the well-to-do of earlier ages.

All these accomplishments have not restrained the advocates of despotism and planning. However, it would have been preposterous for the champions of totalitarianism to disclose the inextricable dictatorial consequences of their endeavors openly. In the nineteenth century the ideas of liberty and the rule of law had won such a prestige that it seemed crazy to attack them frankly. Public opinion was firmly convinced that despotism was done for and could never be restored. Was not even the Czar of barbarian Russia forced to abolish serfdom, to establish trial by jury, to grant a limited freedom to the press and to respect the laws?

Thus the socialists resorted to a trick. They continued to discuss the coming dictatorship of the proletariat, i.e., the dictatorship of each socialist author's own ideas, in their esoteric circles. But to the broad public they spoke in a different way. Socialism, they asserted, will bring true and full liberty and democracy. It will remove all kinds of compulsion and coercion. The state will "wither away." In the socialist commonwealth of the future there will be neither judges and policemen nor prisons and gallows.

But the Bolshevists took off the mask. They were fully convinced that the day of their final and unshakeable victory had dawned. Further dissimulation was neither possible nor required. The gospel of bloodshed could be preached openly. It found an enthusiastic response among all the degenerate literati and parlour intellectuals who for many years already had raved about the writings of Sorel and Nietzsche. The fruits of the "treason of the intellectuals"[1] mellowed to maturity. The youths who had been fed the ideas of Carlyle and Ruskin were ready to seize the reins.

Lenin was not the first usurper. Many tyrants had preceded him. But his predecessors were in conflict with the ideas held by their most eminent contemporaries. They were opposed by public opinion because their principles of government were at variance with

---

[1] Cf. Benda, *La trahison des clercs* (Paris 1927).

the accepted principles of right and legality. They were scorned and detested as usurpers. But Lenin's usurpation was seen in a different light. He was the brutal superman for whose coming the pseudo-philosophers had yearned. He was the counterfeit-savior whom history had elected to bring salvation through bloodshed. Was he not the most orthodox adept of Marxian "scientific" socialism? Was he not the man destined to realize the socialist plans for whose execution the weak statesmen of the decaying democracies were too timid? All well-intentioned people asked for socialism; science, through the mouths of the infallible professors, recommended it; the churches preached Christian socialism; the workers longed for the abolition of the wage system. Here was the man to fulfill all these wishes. He was judicious enough to know that you cannot make an omelet without breaking eggs.

Half a century ago all civilized people had censured Bismarck when he declared that history's great problems must be solved by blood and iron. Now the immense majority of quasi-civilized men bowed to the dictator who was prepared to shed much more blood than Bismarck ever did.

This was the true meaning of the Lenin revolution. All the traditional ideas of right and legality were overthrown. The rule of unrestrained violence and usurpation was substituted for the rule of law. The "narrow horizon of bourgeois legality," as Marx had dubbed it, was abandoned. Henceforth no laws could any longer limit the power of the elect. They were free to kill *ad libitum*. Man's innate impulses toward violent extermination of all whom he dislikes, repressed by a long and wearisome evolution, burst forth. The demons were unfettered. A new age, the age of the usurpers, dawned. The gangsters were called to action, and they listened to the Voice.

Of course, Lenin did not mean this. He did not want to concede to other people the prerogatives which he claimed for himself. He did not want to assign to other men the privilege of liquidating their adversaries. Him alone had history elected and entrusted with the dictatorial power. He was the only "legitimate" dictator because — an inner voice had told him so. Lenin was not bright enough to anticipate that other people, imbued with other creeds, could be bold enough to pretend that they also were called by an

67

inner voice. Yet, within a few years two such men, Mussolini and Hitler, became quite conspicuous.

It is important to realize that Fascism and Nazism were socialist dictatorships. The communists, both the registered members of the communist parties and the fellow-travellers, stigmatize Fascism and Nazism as the highest and last and most depraved stage of capitalism. This is in perfect agreement with their habit of calling every party which does not unconditionally surrender to the dictates of Moscow — even the German Social Democrats, the classical party of Marxism — hirelings of capitalism.

It is of much greater consequence that the communists have succeeded in changing the semantic connotation of the term Fascism. Fascism, as will be shown later, was a variety of Italian socialism. It was adjusted to the particular conditions of the masses in overpopulated Italy. It was not a product of Mussolini's mind and will survive the fall of Mussolini. The foreign policies of Fascism and Nazism, from their early beginnings, were rather opposed to one another. The fact that the Nazis and the Fascists closely cooperated after the Ethiopian war and were allies in the Second World War did not eradicate the differences between these two tenets any more than did the alliance between Russia and the United States eradicate the differences between Sovietism and the American economic system. Fascism and Nazism were both committed to the Soviet principle of dictatorship and violent oppression of dissenters. If one wants to assign Fascism and Nazism to the same class of political systems, one must call this class *dictatorial regime* and one must not neglect to assign the Soviets to the same class.

In recent years the communists' semantic innovations have gone even farther. They call everybody whom they dislike, every advocate of the free enterprise system, a Fascist. Bolshevism, they say, is the only really democratic system. All non-communist countries and parties are essentially undemocratic and Fascist.

It is true that sometimes also non-socialists — the last vestiges of the old aristocracy — toyed with the idea of an aristocratic revolution modelled according to the pattern of Soviet dictatorship. Lenin had opened their eyes. What dupes, they moaned, have we been. We have let ourselves be deluded by the spurious catchwords of the liberal bourgeoisie. We believed that it is not permissible to deviate from the rule of law and to crush mercilessly those challenging our rights. How silly were these Romanovs in granting to their deadly foes the benefits of a fair legal trial! If somebody arouses the suspicion of Lenin, he is done for. Lenin does not hesitate to exterminate, without any trial, not only every suspect, but all his kin and friends too. But the Czars were superstitiously afraid of infringing the rules established by those scraps of paper called laws. When Alexander Ulyanov conspired against the Czar's life, he alone was executed; his brother Vladimir was spared. Thus Alexander III himself preserved the life of Ulyanov-Lenin, the man who ruthlessly exterminated his son, his daughter-in-law and their children and with them all the other members of the family he could catch. Was this not the most stupid and suicidal policy?

However, no action could result from the day dreams of these old Tories. They were a small group of powerless grumblers. They were not backed by any ideological forces and they had no followers.

The idea of such an aristocratic revolution motivated the German *Stahlhelm* and the French *Cagoulards*. The Stahlhelm was simply dispelled by order of Hitler. The French Government could easily imprison the Cagoulards before they had any opportunity to do harm.

Horthy was not a dictator. He was a Regent with a parliamentary government. The Hungarian parliament outlawed communism, but it was jealous in safeguarding its constitutional prerogatives against the Regent and the cabinet.

The nearest approach to an aristocratic dictatorship is Franco's regime. But Franco was merely a puppet of Mussolini and Hitler, who wanted to secure Spanish aid for the impending war against France or at least Spanish "friendly" neutrality. With his protectors gone, his days are numbered.

Dictatorship and violent oppression of all dissenters are today exclusively socialist institutions. This becomes clear as we take a closer look at Fascism and Nazism.

7

Fascism

WHEN the war broke out in 1914, the Italian socialist party was divided as to the policy to be adopted.

One group clung to the rigid principles of Marxism. This war, they maintained, is a war of the capitalists. It is not seemly for the proletarians to side with any of the belligerent parties. The proletarians must wait for the great revolution, the civil war of the united socialists against the united exploiters. They must stand for Italian neutrality.

The second group was deeply affected by the traditional hatred of Austria. In their opinion the first task of the Italians was to free their unredeemed brethren. Only then would the day of the socialist revolution appear.

In this conflict Benito Mussolini, the outstanding man in Italian socialism, chose at first the orthodox Marxian position. Nobody could surpass Mussolini in Marxian zeal. He was the intransigent champion of the pure creed, the unyielding defender of the rights of the exploited proletarians, the eloquent prophet of the socialist bliss to come. He was an adamant adversary of patriotism, nationalism, imperialism, monarchical rule and all religious creeds. When Italy in 1911 opened the great series of wars by an insidious assault upon Turkey, Mussolini organized violent demonstrations against the departure of troops for Libya. Now, in 1914, he branded the war against Germany and Austria as an imperialist war. He was then still under the dominating influence of Angelica Balabanoff, the daughter of a wealthy Russian land owner. Miss Balabanoff had initiated him into the subtleties of Marxism. In her eyes the defeat of the Romanovs counted more than the defeat of the Hapsburgs. She had no sympathies for the ideals of the Risorgimento.

But the Italian intellectuals were first of all nationalists. As in all other European countries, most of the Marxians longed for war and conquest. Mussolini was not prepared to lose his popularity. The thing he hated most was not to be on the side of the victorious faction. He changed his mind and became the most fanatical advocate of Italy's attack on Austria. With French financial aid he founded a newspaper to fight for the cause of the war.

The anti-Fascists blame Mussolini for this defection from the teachings of rigid Marxism. He was bribed, they say, by the French. Now, even these people should know, that the publication of a newspaper requires funds. They themselves do not speak of bribery if a wealthy American provides a man with the money needed for the publication of a fellow-traveller newspaper or if funds mysteriously flow into the communist publishing firms. It is a fact that Mussolini entered the scene of world politics as an ally of the democracies, while Lenin entered it as a virtual ally of imperial Germany.

More than anybody else Mussolini was instrumental in achieving Italy's entry into the first World War. His journalistic propaganda made it possible for the government to declare war on Austria. Only those few people have a right to find fault with his attitude in the years 1914 to 1918 who realize that the disintegration of the Austro-Hungarian Empire spelled the doom of Europe. Only those Italians are free to blame Mussolini who begin to understand that the only means of protecting the Italian-speaking minorities in the littoral districts of Austria against the threatening annihilation by the Slavonic majorities was to preserve the integrity of the Austrian state, whose constitution guaranteed equal rights to all linguistic groups. Mussolini was one of the most wretched figures of history, a ridiculous braggart and swaggerer. But the fact remains that his first great political deed still meets with the approval of all his countrymen and of the immense majority of his foreign detractors.

When the war came to an end, Mussolini's popularity dwindled. The communists, swept into popularity by events in Russia, carried on. But the great communist venture, the occupation of the factories in 1920, ended in complete failure, and the disappointed masses remembered the former leader of the socialist party. They

71

flocked to Mussolini's new party, the Fascists. The youth greeted with turbulent enthusiasm the self-styled successor of the Caesars. Mussolini boasted in later years that he had saved Italy from the danger of communism. His foes passionately dispute his claims. Communism, they say, was no longer a real factor in Italy when Mussolini seized power. The truth is that the frustration of communism swelled the ranks of the Fascists and made it possible for them to destroy all other parties. The overwhelming victory of the Fascists was not the cause, but the consequence of the communist fiasco.

The program of the Fascists, as drafted in 1919, was vehemently anticapitalistic.[1] The most radical New Dealers and even communists could agree with it. When the Fascists came to power, they had forgotten those points of their program which referred to the liberty of thought and the press and the right of assembly. In this respect they were conscientious disciples of Bukharin and Lenin. Moreover they did not suppress, as they had promised, the industrial and financial corporations. Italy badly needed foreign credits for the development of its industries. The main problem for Fascism, in the first years of its rule, was to win the confidence of the foreign bankers. It would have been suicidal to destroy the Italian corporations.

Fascist economic policy did not — at the beginning — essentially differ from those of all other Western nations. It was a policy of interventionism. As the years went on, it more and more approached the Nazi pattern of socialism. When Italy, after the defeat of France, entered the second World War, its economy was by and large already shaped according to the Nazi pattern. The main difference was that the Fascists were less efficient and even more corrupt than the Nazis.

But Mussolini could not long remain without an economic philosophy of his own invention. Fascism posed as a new philosophy, unheard of before and unknown to all other nations. It claimed to be the gospel which the resurrected spirit of ancient Rome brought to the decaying democratic peoples whose barbarian ancestors had once destroyed the Roman empire. It was the consummation both

---

[1] This program is reprinted in English in Count Carlo Sforza's book *Contemporary Italy* (translated by Drake and Denise de Kay, New York 1944), pp. 295-296.

of the Rinascimento and the Risorgimento in every respect, the final liberation of the Latin genius from the yoke of foreign ideologies. Its shining leader, the peerless Duce, was called to find the ultimate solution for the burning problems of society's economic organization and of social justice.

From the dust-heap of discarded socialist utopias, the Fascist scholars salvaged the scheme of guild socialism. Guild socialism was very popular with British socialists in the last years of the first World War and in the first years following the Armistice. It was so impracticable that it disappeared very soon from socialist literature. No serious statesman ever paid any attention to the contradictory and confused plans of guild socialism. It was almost forgotten when the Fascists attached to it a new label and flamboyantly proclaimed *corporativism* as the new social panacea. The public inside and outside of Italy was captivated. Innumerable books, pamphlets and articles were written in praise of the *stato corporativo*. The governments of Austria and Portugal very soon declared that they were committed to the noble principles of corporativism. The papal encyclical *Quadragesimo Anno* (1931) contained some paragraphs which could be interpreted — but need not be — as an approval of corporativism. In France its ideas found many eloquent supporters.

It was mere idle talk. Never did the Fascists make any attempt to realize the corporativist program, industrial self-government. They changed the name of the chambers of commerce into corporative councils. They called *corporazione* the compulsory organizations of the various branches of industry which were the administrative units for the execution of the German pattern of socialism they had adopted. But there was no question of the *corporazione's* self-government. The Fascist cabinet did not tolerate anybody's interference with its absolute authoritarian control of production. All the plans for the establishment of the corporative system remained a dead letter.

Italy's main problem is its comparative overpopulation. In this age of barriers to trade and migration the Italians are condemned to subsist permanently on a lower standard of living than that of the inhabitants of the countries more favored by nature. The Fascists saw only one means to remedy this unfortunate situation: conquest. They were too narrow-minded to comprehend that the redress they recommended was spurious and worse than the evil. They were moreover so entirely blinded by self-conceit and vainglory that they failed to realize that their provocative speeches were simply ridiculous. The foreigners whom they insolently challenged knew very well how negligible Italy's military forces were.

Fascism was not, as its advocates boasted, an original product of the Italian mind. It began with a split in the ranks of Marxian socialism, which certainly was an imported doctrine. Its economic program was borrowed from German non-Marxian socialism and its aggressiveness was likewise copied from Germans, the *Alldeutsche* or Pan-German forerunners of the Nazis. Its conduct of government affairs was a replica of Lenin's dictatorship. Corporativism, its much advertised ideological adornment, was of British origin. The only home-grown ingredient of Fascism was the theatrical style of its processions, shows and festivals.

The short-lived Fascist episode ended in blood, misery and ignominy. But the forces which generated Fascism are not dead. Fanatical nationalism is a feature common to all present-day Italians. The communists are certainly not prepared to renounce their principle of dictatorial oppression of all dissenters. Neither do the Catholic parties advocate freedom of thought, of the press or of religion. There are in Italy only very few people indeed who comprehend that the indispensable prerequisite of democracy and the rights of men is economic freedom.

It may happen that Fascism will be resurrected very soon under a new label and with new slogans and symbols. But if this happens, the consequences will be detrimental. For Fascism is not as the Fascists trumpeted a "new way to life"[1]; it is a rather old way toward destruction and death.

---

[1] Cf. for instance Mario Palmieri, *The Philosophy of Fascism* (Chicago 1936), p. 248.

8

Nazism

THE philosophy of the Nazis, the *German National Socialist Labor Party,* is the purest and most consistent manifestation of the anticapitalistic and socialistic spirit of our age. Its essential ideas are not German or "Aryan" in origin, nor are they peculiar to the present-day Germans. In the genealogical tree of the Nazi doctrine such Latins as Sismondi and Georges Sorel, and such Anglo-Saxons as Carlyle, Ruskin and Houston Stewart Chamberlain, were more conspicuous than any German. Even the best known ideological attire of Nazism, the fable of the superiority of the Aryan master race, was not of German provenance; its author was a Frenchman, Gobineau. Germans of Jewish descent, like Lassalle, Lasson, Stahl, and Walter Rathenau, contributed more to the essential tenets of Nazism than such men as Sombart, Spann and Ferdinand Fried. The slogan into which the Nazis condensed their economic philosophy, viz., *Gemeinnutz geht vor Eigennutz,* (i.e., the commonweal ranks above private profit,) is likewise the idea underlying the American New Deal and the Soviet management of economic affairs. It implies that profit-seeking business harms the vital interests of the immense majority and that it is the sacred duty of popular government to prevent the emergence of profits by public control of production and distribution.

The only specifically German ingredient in Nazism was its striving after the conquest of *Lebensraum.* And this too was an outcome of their agreement with the ideas guiding the policies of the most influential political parties of all other countries. These parties proclaim income equality as the main thing. The Nazis do the same. What characterizes the Nazis is the fact that they are not prepared to acquiesce in a state of affairs in which the Germans are doomed for ever to be "imprisoned," as they say, in a comparatively small and overpopulated area in which the productivity of labor must be smaller than in the comparatively underpopulated countries, much better endowed with natural resources. They aim at a fairer distribution of the earth's natural resources. As a "have-not" nation they look at the wealth of the richer nations with the same feelings with which many people in the Western countries look at the higher incomes of some of their countrymen. The "progressives" in the Anglo-Saxon countries assert that "liberty is not worth having" for those who are wronged by the comparative smallness of their incomes. The Nazis say the same with regard to international relations. In their opinion the only freedom that matters is *Nahrungsfreiheit,* (viz., freedom from importing food). They aim at the acquisition of a territory so large and rich in natural resources that they could live in economic self-sufficiency at a standard not lower than that of any other nation. They consider themselves as revolutionaries fighting for their inalienable natural rights against the vested interests of a host of reactionary nations.

It is easy for economists to explode the fallacies involved in the Nazi doctrines. But those who disparage economics as "orthodox and reactionary" and fanatically support the spurious creeds of socialism and economic nationalism were at a loss to refute them. For Nazism was nothing but the logical application of their own tenets to the particular conditions of comparatively overpopulated Germany.

For more than seventy years the German professors of political science, history, law, geography and philosophy eagerly imbued their disciples with a hysterical hatred of capitalism and preached the war of "liberation" against the capitalistic West. The German "socialists of the chair," much admired in all foreign countries, were the pacemakers of the two World Wars. At the turn of the century the immense majority of the Germans were already radical supporters of socialism and aggressive nationalism. They were then already firmly committed to the principles of Nazism. What was lacking and was added later was only the term to signify their doctrine.

When the Soviet policies of mass extermination of all dissenters and of ruthless violence removed the inhibitions against wholesale murder, which still troubled some of the Germans, nothing could any longer stop the advance of Nazism. The Nazis were quick to adopt the Soviet methods. They imported from Russia: the one party system and the preeminence of this party in political life; the paramount position assigned to the secret police; the concentration camps; the administrative execution or imprisonment of all opponents; the extermination of the families of suspects and of exiles; the methods of propaganda; the organization of affiliated parties abroad and their employment for fighting their governments and for espionage and sabotage; the use of the diplomatic and consular service for fomenting revolution; and many other things besides. There were nowhere more docile disciples of Lenin, Trotsky and Stalin than the Nazis were.

Hitler was not the founder of Nazism; he was its product. He was, like most of his collaborators, a sadistic gangster. He was uneducated and ignorant; he had failed even in the lower grades of high school. He never had any honest job. It is a fable that he had ever been a paperhanger. His military career in the first World War was rather mediocre. The First Class Iron Cross was given to him after the end of the war as a reward for his activities as a political agent. He was a maniac obsessed by megalomania. But learned professors nourished his self-conceit. Werner Sombart, who once had boasted that his life was devoted to the task of fighting for the ideas of Marx,[1] Sombart, whom the American Economic Association had elected to Honorary Membership and many non-German universities to honorary degrees, candidly declared that *Führertum* means a permanent revelation and that the *Führer* receives his orders directly from God, the supreme *Führer* of the Universe.[2]

The Nazi plan was more comprehensive and therefore more pernicious than that of the Marxians. It aimed at abolishing laissez-faire not only in the production of material goods, but no less in the production of men. The Führer was not only the general manager of all industries; he was also the general manager of the breeding-farm intent upon rearing superior men and eliminating in-

---

[1] Sombart, *Das Lebenswerk von Karl Marx,* (Jena 1909), p. 3. .

[2] Sombart, *A New Social Philosophy,* translated and edited by K. F. Geiser (Princeton University Press 1937), p. 194.

ferior stock. A grandiose scheme of eugenics was to be put into effect according to "scientific" principles.

It is vain for the champions of eugenics to protest that they did not mean what the Nazis executed. Eugenics aims at placing some men, backed by the police power, in complete control of human reproduction. It suggests that the methods applied to domestic animals be applied to men. This is precisely what the Nazis tried to do. The only objection which a consistent eugenist can raise is that his own plan differs from that of the Nazi scholars and that he wants to rear another type of men than the Nazis. As every supporter of economic planning aims at the execution of his own plan only, so every advocate of eugenic planning aims at the execution of his own plan and wants himself to act as the breeder of human stock.

The eugenists pretend that they want to eliminate criminal individuals. But the qualification of a man as a criminal depends upon the prevailing laws of the country and varies with the change in social and political ideologies. Joan d'Arc, John Huss, Giordano Bruno and Galileo Galilei were criminals from the point of view of the laws which their judges applied. When Stalin robbed the Russian State Bank of several million rubles, he committed a crime. Today it is an offense in Russia to disagree with Stalin. In Nazi Germany sexual intercourse between "Aryans" and the members of an "inferior" race was a crime. Whom do the eugenists want to eliminate, Brutus or Caesar? Both violated the laws of their country. If 18th century eugenists had prevented alcohol addicts from generating children, their planning would have eliminated Beethoven.

It must be emphasized again: there is no such thing as a scientific *ought*. Which men are superior and which are inferior can only be decided by personal value judgments not liable to verification or falsification. The eugenists delude themselves in assuming that they themselves will be called to decide what qualities are to be conserved in the human stock. They are too dull to take into account the possibility that other people might make the choice according to their own value judgments.[1] In the eyes of the Nazis

---

[1] Cf. the devastating critique of racial eugenics by H. S. Jennings, *The Biological Basis of Human Nature*, (New York 1930), pp. 223-252.

the brutal killer, the "fair-haired beast," is the most perfect specimen of mankind.

The mass slaughters perpetrated in the Nazi horror camps are too horrible to be adequately described by words. But they were the logical and consistent application of doctrines and policies parading as applied science and approved by some men who in a sector of the natural sciences have displayed acumen and technical skill in laboratory research.

9

The Teachings of Soviet Experience

MANY people all over the world assert that the Soviet "experiment" has supplied conclusive evidence in favor of socialism and disproved all, or at least most, of the objections raised against it. The facts, they say, speak for themselves. It is no longer permissible to pay any attention to the spurious aprioristic reasoning of armchair economists criticizing the socialist plans. A crucial experiment has exploded their fallacies.

It is, first of all, necessary to comprehend that in the field of purposive human action and social relations no experiments can be made and no experiments have ever been made. The experimental method to which the natural sciences owe all their achievements is inapplicable in the social sciences. The natural sciences are in a position to observe in the laboratory experiment the consequences of the isolated change in one element only while other elements remain unchanged. Their experimental observation refers ultimately to certain isolable elements in sense experience. What the natural sciences call facts are the causal relations shown in such experiments. Their theories and hypotheses must be in agreement with these facts.

But the experience with which the social sciences have to deal is essentially different. It is historical experience. It is an experience of complex phenomena, of the joint effects brought about by the cooperation of a multiplicity of elements. The social sciences are never in a position to control the conditions of change and to isolate them from one another in the way in which the experimenter proceeds in arranging his experiments. They never enjoy the advantage of observing the consequences of a change in one element only, other conditions being equal. They are never faced with facts in the sense in which the natural sciences employ this term. Every fact and every experience with which the social sciences have to deal is open to various interpretations. Historical facts and historical experience can never prove or disprove a statement in the way in which an experiment proves or disproves.

Historical experience never comments upon itself. It needs to be interpreted from the point of view of theories constructed without the aid of experimental observations. There is no need to enter into an epistemological analysis of the logical and philosophical problems involved. It is enough to refer to the fact that nobody — whether social scientist or layman — ever proceeds otherwise when dealing with historical experience. Every discussion of the relevance and meaning of historical facts falls back very soon on a discussion of abstract general principles, logically antecedent to the facts to be elucidated and interpreted. Reference to historical experience can never solve any problem or answer any question. The same historical events and the same statistical figures are claimed as confirmations of contradictory theories.

If history could prove and teach us anything, it would be that private ownership of the means of production is a necessary requisite of civilization and material well-being. All civilizations have up to now been based on private property. Only nations committed to the principle of private property have risen above penury and produced science, art and literature. There is no experience to show that any other social system could provide mankind with any of the achievements of civilization. Nevertheless, only few people consider this as a sufficient and incontestable refutation of the socialist program.

On the contrary, there are even people who argue the other way round. It is frequently asserted that the system of private property is done for precisely because it was the system that men applied in the past. However beneficial a social system may have been in the past, they say, it cannot be so in the future too; a new age requires a new mode of social organization. Mankind has reached maturity; it would be pernicious for it to cling to the principles to which it resorted in the earlier stages of its evolution. This is certainly the most radical abandonment of experimentalism. The experimental method may assert: because a produced in the past the result *b*, it will produce it in the future also. It must never assert: because *a* produced in the past the result *b*, it is proved that it cannot produce it any longer.

In spite of the fact that mankind has had no experience with the socialist mode of production, the socialist writers have constructed various schemes of socialist systems based on aprioristic reasoning. But as soon as anybody dares to analyze these projects and to scrutinize them with regard to their feasibility and their ability to further human welfare, the socialists vehemently object. These analyses, they say, are merely idle aprioristic speculations. They cannot disprove the correctness of our statements and the expediency of our plans. They are not experimental. One must try socialism and then the results will speak for themselves.

What these socialists ask for is absurd. Carried to its ultimate logical consequences, their idea implies that men are not free to refute by reasoning any scheme, however nonsensical, self-contradictory and impracticable, that any reformer is pleased to suggest. According to their view, the only method permissible for the refutation of such a — necessarily abstract and aprioristic — plan is to test it by reorganizing the whole of society according to its designs. As soon as a man sketches the plan for a better social order, all nations are bound to try it and to see what will happen.

Even the most stubborn socialists cannot fail to admit that there are various plans for the construction of the future utopia, incompatible with one another. There is the Soviet pattern of all-round socialization of all enterprises and their outright bureaucratic management; there is the German pattern of *Zwangswirtschaft,* toward the complete adoption of which the Anglo-Saxon countries are manifestly tending; there is guild socialism, under the name of corporativism still very popular in some Catholic countries. There are many other varieties. The supporters of most of these competing schemes assert that the beneficial results to be expected from their own scheme will appear only when all nations will have adopted it; they deny that socialism in one country only can already bring the blessings they ascribe to socialism. The Marxians declare that the bliss of socialism will emerge only in its "higher phase" which, as they hint, will appear only after the working class will have passed "through long struggles, through a whole series of historical processes, wholly transforming both circumstances and men."[1] The inference from all this is that one must realize socialism and quietly wait for a very long time until its promised benefits come. No unpleasant experiences in the period of transition, no matter how long this period may be, can disprove the assertion that socialism is the best of all conceivable modes of social organization. He that believeth shall be saved.

But which of the many socialist plans, contradicting one another, should be adopted? Every socialist sect passionately proclaims that its own brand is alone genuine socialism and that all other sects advocate counterfeit, entirely pernicious measures. In fighting one another the various socialist factions resort to the same methods of abstract reasoning which they stigmatize as vain apriorism whenever they are applied against the correctness of their own statements and the expediency and practicability of their own schemes. There is, of course, no other method available. The fallacies implied in a system of abstract reasoning — such as socialism is — cannot be smashed otherwise than by abstract reasoning.

The fundamental objection advanced against the practicability of socialism refers to the impossibility of economic calculation. It has been demonstrated in an irrefutable way that a socialist commonwealth would not be in a position to apply economic calculation. Where there are no market prices for the factors of production because they are neither bought nor sold, it is impossible to resort to calculation in planning future action and in determining the result of past action. A socialist management of production would simply not know whether or not what it plans and executes is the most appropriate means to attain the ends sought. It will operate in the dark, as it were. It will squander the scarce factors of production both material and human (labor). Chaos and poverty for all will unavoidably result.

All earlier socialists were too narrow-minded to see this essential point. Neither did the earlier economists conceive its full importance. When the present writer in 1920 showed the impossibility of economic calculation under socialism, the apologists of socialism embarked upon the search for a method of calculation applicable to a socialist system. They utterly failed in these endeav-

---

[1] Cf. Marx, *Der Bürgerkrieg in Frankreich*, ed. by Pfemfert (Berlin 1919), p. 54.

83

ors. The futility of the schemes they produced could easily be shown. Those communists who were not entirely intimidated by the fear of the Soviet executioners, for instance Trotsky, freely admitted that economic accounting is unthinkable without market relations.[1] The intellectual bankruptcy of the socialist doctrine can no longer be disguised. In spite of its unprecedented popularity, socialism is done for. No economist can any longer question its impracticability. The avowal of socialist ideas is today the proof of a complete ignorance of the basic problems of economics. The socialists' claims are as vain as those of the astrologers and the magicians.

With regard to this essential problem of socialism, viz., economic calculation, the Russian "experiment" is of no avail. The Soviets are operating within a world the greater part of which still clings to a market economy. They base the calculations on which they make their decisions on the prices established abroad. Without the help of these prices their actions would be aimless and planless. Only as far as they refer to this foreign price system are they able to calculate, keep books and prepare their plans. In this respect one may agree with the statement of various socialist and communist authors that socialism in one or a few countries only is not yet true socialism. Of course, these authors attach a quite different meaning to their assertion. They want to say that the full blessings of socialism can be reaped only in a world-embracing socialist community. Those familiar with the teachings of economics must, on the contrary, recognize that socialism will result in full chaos precisely if it is applied in the greater part of the world.

The second main objection raised against socialism is that it is a less efficient mode of production than is capitalism and that it will impair the productivity of labor. Consequently, in a socialist commonwealth the standard of living of the masses will be low when compared with conditions prevailing under capitalism. There is no doubt that this objection has not been disproved by the Soviet experience. The only certain fact about Russian affairs under the Soviet regime with regard to which all people agree is:

---

[1] Cf. Hayek, *The Use of Knowledge in Society* (The American Economic Review, 1945), Vol. XXXV, pp. 528-530.

that the standard of living of the Russian masses is much lower than that of the masses in the country which is universally considered as the paragon of capitalism, the United States of America. If we were to regard the Soviet regime as an experiment, we would have to say that the experiment has clearly demonstrated the superiority of capitalism and the inferiority of socialism.

It is true that the advocates of socialism are intent upon interpreting the lowness of the Russian standard of living in a different way. As they see things, it was not caused by socialism, but was — in spite of socialism — brought about by other agencies. They refer to various factors, e.g., the poverty of Russia under the Czars, the disastrous effects of the wars, the alleged hostility of the capitalist democratic nations, the alleged sabotage of the remnants of the Russian aristocracy and bourgeoisie and of the Kulaks. There is no need to enter into an examination of these matters. For we do not contend that any historical experience could prove or disprove a theoretical statement in the way in which a crucial experiment can verify or falsify a statement concerning natural events. It is not the critics of socialism, but its fanatical advocates who maintain that the Soviet "experiment" proves something with regard to the effects of socialism. However, what they are really doing in dealing with the manifest and undisputed facts of Russian experience is to push them aside by impermissible tricks and fallacious syllogisms. They disavow the obvious facts by commenting upon them in such a way as to deny their bearing and their significance upon the question to be answered.

Let us, for the sake of argument, assume that their interpretation is correct. But then it would still be absurd to assert that the Soviet experiment has evidenced the superiority of socialism. All that could be said is: the fact that the masses' standard of living is low in Russia does not provide conclusive evidence that socialism is inferior to capitalism.

A comparison with experimentation in the field of the natural sciences may clarify the issue. A biologist wants to test a new patent food. He feeds it to a number of guinea pigs. They all lose weight and finally die. The experimenter believes that their decline and death were not caused by the patent food, but by merely accidental affliction with pneumonia. It would nevertheless be absurd for him to proclaim that his experiment had evidenced the nutritive value of the compound because the unfavorable result is to be ascribed to accidental occurrences, not causally linked with the experimental arrangement. The best he could contend is that the outcome of the experiment was not conclusive, that it does not prove anything *against* the nutritive value of the food tested. Things are, he could assert, as if no experiment had been tried at all.

Even if the Russian masses' standard of living were much higher than that of the capitalist countries, this still would not be conclusive proof of the superiority of socialism. It may be admitted that the undisputed fact that the standard of living in Russia is lower than that in the capitalist West does not conclusively prove the inferiority of socialism. But it is nothing short of idiocy to announce that the experience of Russia has demonstrated the superiority of public control of production.

Neither does the fact that the Russian armies, after having suffered many defeats, finally — with armament manufactured by American big business and donated to them by the American taxpayers — could aid the Americans in the conquest of Germany prove the preeminence of communism. When the British forces had to sustain a temporary reverse in North Africa, Professor Harold Laski, that most radical advocate of socialism, was quick to announce the final failure of capitalism. He was not consistent enough to interpret the German conquest of the Ukraine as the final failure of Russian communism. Neither did he retract his condemnation of the British system when his country emerged victorious from the war. If the military events are to be considered as the proof of any social system's excellence, it is rather the American than the Russian system for which they bear witness.

Nothing that has happened in Russia since 1917 contradicts any of the statements of the critics of socialism and communism. Even if one bases one's judgment exclusively on the writings of communists and fellow-travellers, one cannot discover any feature in Russian conditions that tells in favor of the Soviet's social and political system. All the technological improvements of the last decades originated in the capitalistic countries. It is true that the Russians have tried to copy some of these innovations. But so did all backward oriental peoples too.

Some communists are eager to have us believe that the ruthless oppression of dissenters and the radical abolition of the freedom of thought, speech and the press are not inherent marks of the public control of business. They are, they argue, only accidental phenomena of communism, its signature in a country which — as was the case with Russia — never enjoyed freedom of thought and conscience. However, these apologists for totalitarian despotism are at a loss to explain how the rights of men could be safeguarded under government omnipotence.

Freedom of thought and conscience is a sham in a country in which the authorities are free to exile everybody whom they dislike into the Arctic or the desert and to assign him hard labor for life. The autocrat may always try to justify such arbitrary acts by pretending that they are motivated exclusively by considerations of public welfare and economic expediency. He alone is the supreme arbiter to decide all matters referring to the execution of the plan. Freedom of the press is illusory when the government owns and operates all paper mills, printing offices and publishing houses and ultimately decides what is to be printed and what not. The right of assembly is vain if the government owns all assembly halls and determines for what purposes they shall be used. And so it is with all other liberties too. In one of his lucid intervals Trotsky — of course Trotsky the hunted exile, not the ruthless commander of the Red army — saw things realistically and declared: "In a country where the sole employer is the State, opposition means death by slow starvation. The old principle: who does not work shall not eat, has been replaced by a new one: who does not obey shall not eat."[1] This confession settles the issue.

What the Russian experience shows is a very low level of the standard of living of the masses and unlimited dictatorial despotism. The apologists of communism are intent upon explaining these uncontested facts as accidental only; they are, they say, not the fruit of communism, but occurred in spite of communism. But even if one were to accept these excuses for the sake of argument, it would be simply nonsensical to maintain that the Soviet "experiment" has demonstrated anything *in favor* of communism and socialism.

---

[1] Quoted by Hayek, *The Road to Serfdom* (1944), Chapter IX.

IO

The Alleged Inevitability of Socialism

MANY people believe that the coming of totalitarianism is inevitable. The "wave of the future," they say, carries mankind inexorably toward a system under which all human affairs are managed by omnipotent dictators. It is useless to fight against the unfathomable decrees of history.

The truth is that most people lack the intellectual ability and courage to resist a popular movement, however pernicious and ill-considered. Bismarck once deplored the lack of what he called civilian courage, i.e., bravery in dealing with civic affairs on the part of his countrymen. But neither did the citizens of other nations display more courage and judiciousness when faced with the menace of communist dictatorship. They either yielded silently or timidly raised some trifling objections.

One does not fight socialism by criticizing only some accidental features of its schemes. In attacking many socialists' stand on divorce and birth control or their ideas about art and literature, one does not refute socialism. It is not enough to disapprove of the Marxian assertions that the theory of relativity or the philosophy of Bergson or psychoanalysis is "bourgeois" moonshine. Those who find fault with Bolshevism and Nazism only for their anti-Christian leanings implicitly endorse all the rest of these bloody schemes.

On the other hand, it is sheer stupidity to praise the totalitarian regimes for alleged achievements which have no reference whatever to their political and economic principles. It is questionable whether the observations that in Fascist Italy the railroad trains ran on schedule and the bug population of second-rate hotel beds was decreasing, were correct or not; but it is in any case of no importance for the problem of Fascism. The fellow-travellers are enraptured by Russian films, Russian music and Russian caviar. But there lived greater musicians in other countries and under other social systems; good pictures were produced in other countries too; and it is certainly not a merit of Generalissimo Stalin that the taste of caviar is delicious. Neither does the prettiness of Russian ballet dancers or the construction of a great power station on the Dnieper expiate for the mass slaughter of the Kulaks .

The readers of picture magazines and the movie-fans long for the picturesque. The operatic pageants of the Fascists and the Nazis and the parading of the girl-battalions of the Red army are after their heart. It is more fun to listen to the radio speeches of a dictator than to study economic treatises. The entrepreneurs and technologists who pave the way for economic improvement work in seclusion; their work is not suitable to be visualized on the screen. But the dictators, intent upon spreading death and destruction, are spectacularly in sight of the public. Dressed in military garb they eclipse in the eyes of the moviegoers the colourless bourgeois in plain clothes.

The problems of society's economic organization are not suitable for light talk at fashionable cocktail parties. Neither can they be dealt with adequately by demagogues haranguing mass assemblies. They are serious things. They require painstaking studies. They must not be taken lightly.

The socialist propaganda never encountered any decided opposition. The devastating critique by which the economists exploded the futility and impracticability of the socialist schemes and doctrines did not reach the moulders of public opinion. The universities were mostly dominated by socialist or interventionist pedants not only in continental Europe, where they were owned and operated by the governments, but even in the Anglo-Saxon countries. The politicians and the statesmen, anxious not to lose popularity, were lukewarm in their defense of freedom. The policy of appeasement, so much criticized when applied in the case of the Nazis and the Fascists, was practised universally for many decades with regard to all other brands of socialism. It was this defeatism that made the rising generation believe that the victory of socialism is inevitable.

It is not true that the masses are vehemently asking for socialism and that there is no means to resist them. The masses favor socialism because they trust the socialist propaganda of the intellectuals. The intellectuals, not the populace, are moulding public opinion. It is a lame excuse of the intellectuals that they must yield to the masses. They themselves have generated the socialist ideas and indoctrinated the masses with them. No proletarian or son of a proletarian has contributed to the elaboration of the interventionist and socialist programs. Their authors were all of bourgeois background. The esoteric writings of dialectical materialism, of Hegel, the father both of Marxism and of German aggressive nationalism, the books of Georges Sorel, of Gentile and of Spengler were not read by the average man; they did not move the masses directly. It was the intellectuals who popularized them.

The intellectual leaders of the peoples have produced and propagated the fallacies which are on the point of destroying liberty and Western civilization. The intellectuals alone are responsible for the mass slaughters which are the characteristic mark of our century. They alone can reverse the trend and pave the way for a resurrection of freedom.

Not mythical "material productive forces," but reason and ideas determine the course of human affairs. What is needed to stop the trend toward socialism and despotism is common-sense and moral courage.

THE FOUNDATION FOR
ECONOMIC EDUCATION, INC.
IRVINGTON-ON-HUDSON, NEW YORK

PRINTED IN U.S.A.